This second edition is dedicated to
those who believe in Afrikan Nationhood and who
live through spirit.

For Hanifah
Live your dream to the
fullest extent.
Peace + ancestral
guidance

SPIRITED WOMEN

Lessons in Living

Olayinka Ayoade

Olayinka Ayoade

1st July 2005.

African Remembrance
Day.

With a new foreword by Caroline Shola Arewa
Author of 'Opening to Spirit'

Published by
Black Ankh Publications
London

Black Ankh Publications
P.O. Box 36089
London SW16 6WF

Copyright © 1996 Olayinka Ayoade
First Printing 1998

Cover Artwork, Concept and Design by Alvin Kofi
Editing by Ras Kwende Anbessa-Ebanks

ISBN 0-9544277-0-X

Second Edition Published 2003

CONTENTS

*You are a woman of unlimited potential, undefined by
place or time. By increasing your knowledge of the
women who came before you and who lived victorious
lives, you too can be inspired to live spiritedly.*

RELATING TO OTHERS

*Our Mothers are the backbone of our communities.
They are a tireless source of strength and love. Give
thanks for the Mothers in your life and recognise
their contribution to the development of those they
have nurtured.*

*The Afrikan man is your natural mate. The Afrikan
man is your natural companion. Treat him as such,
and give him the support and love that he needs to
reach his full potential.*

*Within each sistah you should see a representation of
yourself. Therefore, greet each sistah that you meet in
a spirit of friendship and trust. Share your knowledge
with her and encourage her to be the best that she can
be, even as she does the same for you.*

your scars. If you deny your own growth through fear of the unknown, you are contributing to your own stumbling blocks, in which case you can blame nobody but yourself.

Acknowledgements

When I first wrote Spirited Women back in 1995 I had wanted to acknowledge and give thanks to those forces, which have influenced and guided me in my journey through life. I chickened out, daunted by the task of making coherent thoughts which are heavily tied up in my being and sometimes difficult to articulate. For this edition I was determined to say thank you in a way which fully communicates the depth of my regard for those named.

I give thanks to the Creator of all things, for the power of his/her love and benevolence, guidance and care in good times and bad. Adupe, ase (thanks, power) Oludamare, without your presence nothing is possible. I give thanks that you empowered me to deliver this work; your presence in my life is my inspiration. Adupe to my ancestors who guide and protect me. Your power knows no bounds, I salute you for all you have done in the past and continue to do in the future. Thanks to my Mother who blessed her six children with sound moral values and the drive to achieve. Thanks to my siblings who are always there for me, each in their own unique way.

The deepest thanks to my sistah-friend Asha for her laughter and the courage to always voice her honest opinion. Respect to Mayemi who leads by example. For Vicki and Claire who offer me unlimited faith. Thanks to Elaine for being there. For Ngozi Awa who always has an open door. For Achieng, Foluso & Jumoke who helped me to ride the Namibian storm. Adupe to Bola my spiritual sistah who reminds me of the power of the spoken word. For my children Kunle and Aduke who show me my true character every day. Thank you for choosing me. And lastly, for Ifagbemi Ajani, who can inspire the brightest feelings from the darkest day.

One Love

Foreword by
Caroline Shola Arewa
Author of 'Opening to Spirit'

We are living in a time of major acceleration and spiritual growth. I am privileged in my work as a Spiritual guide, Healer, Author, International Speaker and Life Coach to meet many amazing souls as they unfold into their greatness. Today, more than any other time, people are eagerly seeking spiritual guidance, wisdom and love.

People are awakening as if from a long sleep and asking many questions. We are no longer content to drift through life not quite knowing why we are here. We desire inner, over and under standing. We want to fully appreciate our unique life purpose. We want to step into our power and our richness utilising the gifts bestowed on us by our Creator. Somehow life and its many lessons are showing us the importance of 'opening to spirit'.

Olayinka Ayoade is a 'Spirited Women' with a Divine message. A sistah who has taken the lessons life handed her and woven them into brightly coloured, beautifully textured, teachings. Her intention in these pages is to enrich the lives of people everywhere especially our African Brothas and Sistahs. Her desire is to improve communication, raise important issues and share her love of living with others.

While living and working in Namibia, spirit so filled Olayinka's life that it overflowed and allowed her to pen this inspirational book. I know from my experience of travelling in Africa and Asia just how powerful taking time to slow your pace of living can actually be. My life was completely transformed by the opportunity of learning ancient ways first hand. But it is not always necessary to take an outer journey to be transformed within. We all know the challenges life presents. And the obstacles we face as we pass through life. We know pain and we know adversity but most of all we know we can rise above all life's difficulties when we tune to our Divine Spiritual Self.

Olayinka urges us to be guided by Spirit and recognise some simple but powerful teachings. Teaching that relate to many aspects of living such as, the choices we make in life, our success, discipline, and parenting skills. Olayinka shows us we can find self-love, let go of negativity and embrace life's song. The book is highlighted with affirmations and poems. '*You are beautiful to me*' are words from the poem '*Smiles Within*', it is one of my favourite poems in the book. It speaks of a sensuality and beauty we all know.

You have been guided to this book at a special time in your life. This book was written because Spirit is calling our attention, because change is desperately needed. It is a book that uplifts, guides and contributes to our well-being as first world children. Olayinka empowered herself by writing this book and you will be empowered by reading it.

As you read I offer you the prayer that you will find a Divine message in these words and that you will move forward in your life claiming your 'Spirited Self' and remain forever blessed.

Shola Arewa
Author of 'Opening to Spirit'
www.shola.co.uk

December 2002

The Source

My sistah, my sistah
tell me the story of your love.
The things, the myriad things
you hoped, dreamed to do.
But love of those in your life
kept you away.

The desires you had to;
Or chose to forsake
again, again and again.
With not a tear to trace
their lost path.

Where? From what source?
From which dark pool of love
do you breathe your resilience?
How is it that you do not falter,
when so many drop,
like flies around you?

When I am near you
I become strengthened.
For your powerful light
casts such a glow of redemption
that my ills flow from me,
ebbing pools of distress
that I could not release alone.

My sistah, my sistah
tell me the story of your love.
That I might find strength
to search for the love that lies
unpossessed within me.

Preface: A Prodigal Daughter Returns

In the summer of 1995, at the age of 25, I took a return journey to my homeland, Afrika, in the hope that I would renew and replenish my belief in my people, my continent and myself. This first trip back home was everything that I imagined it would be. I connected with that land like I had connected with no other before, for I was standing upon my birthright. As I stepped from the plane at Gambia's International Airport, my nose breathed blood in the truest sense of baptism. My blood frothed from my nose with no warning, and splashed onto the tarmac soil of Afrika. I was at once embarrassed, but strangely pleased. Embarrassed, because I was immediately noticeable to many people close by; yet I was proud and pleased because I saw in my bloodied nose, symbolism of a historic return of an Afrikan daughter coming home. I knew deep within my heart, that Mama Afrika recognised my returning. That she wanted to cleanse me in the best possible way, by allowing my life's force to mingle unabashedly with her own, our landmass, Afrika.

The following month that I spent travelling overland, across the west coast of Afrika, from Gambia to Nigeria, crossing eight European constructed country frontiers, awakened me to the tremendous hardships that Afrikan people endure everyday, as well as the tremendous potential that we all hold. My heart grieved for those women and children I saw working so hard. Girls and boys so young, with pots of water nearly as large as themselves, struggled not to drop their loads. Children so young, who should have been in school trying to further themselves and their people, toiled late into the evening. Women, carrying out numerous back-breaking tasks. In the fields: planting, sowing, fetching, and cutting. In their homes: cooking, cleaning, mending, child-caring from dawn 'til dusk. Like sistah Binta, who I met in the Gambia. A woman who, besides her daily tasks as farmer, mother, wife and homemaker, served as a village councillor for six villages in her region. Binta's tasks as a village representative involved her advising the women of the villages on how they could better their lives through businesses, and appropriate farming methods. Binta would also encourage her sistahs to seek representation of their voices at local and national level. Binta's work as a village representative necessitates that she should visit all villages under her care. Typically, in one day Binta would walk six miles, between three villages, in the hot sun, with her one-year-old baby clasped to her back. Binta's work as a women's representative is unpaid. Although in the midst of poverty, she makes her contribution to her community because of her indomitable belief in women's empowerment, despite the many tasks she has to do at home.

No matter where I saw women in Afrika, invariably they would be working. Sadly, I saw too many mothers with their young babies, sitting at too many crossroads late into the night, hoping to sell that last mango, yam, or piece of fried fish, so that she could return home with a few more pennies in her pocket.

Distressingly, I saw many of our Afrikan brothas enjoying the liberty of leisure time, while women and children worked consistently. True, Afrikan men could be found to be working extremely hard in the fields and in the cities. But it was noticeable during all my days travelling through the villages of West Afrika, that I never once saw a group of women sitting under a tree enjoying a game of dominoes, or awari, and drinking a few cool beers. That kind of luxury never appeared to be available to them, even had they wanted it. Sadly, I found it difficult to keep track of whether it was a weekday or the weekend because Afrikan women worked so hard, seven days a week, while some of our men had time to play board games during the afternoon hours of weekdays.

In the economy of Afrika, Afrikan women work too hard, while some of our brothas do not aid us, perhaps because of tradition. This has got to stop for the betterment of Afrika, and all her peoples. I implore you to understand that this book is not a treatise against my brothas. I love Afrikan men for all the beauty that they are capable of bringing to the world, and as the natural and only complement to Afrikan women. But my love for my brotha cannot and should not stop me from speaking truth, speaking out against outdated practices which ultimately contribute to holding back Afrikan women from achieving their great potential.

The genesis of this book can only be fully explained in the context of my first sojourn to Afrika. After my experiences travelling through West Afrika, I was determined to document a tribute to all Afrikan women throughout the world. To contribute in some small way to the upliftment and empowerment of Afrikan women; to encourage all of us to be the best that we can be in all things. I dearly hope that Afrikan women, who honour me by reading this book, find something that will aid them in their search for self-empowerment. I sincerely hope that each brotha who reads this book finds knowledge which will assist him in understanding, and appreciating the sistahs in his life.

It has been a pure pleasure for me to write this book, because writing about the spirit of Afrikan women is like drinking from the well of life, over and over again. Each revisit more splendid than the one before.

Life's Song

My passage to this life
has been thwart with difficulties
and turmoil, challenges and
realisations of substance
beyond my control.

Substances which instead
frequently mould me to the woman
I am today.
Steeped in tradition my life is carved.
Echoing the lives of my people gone,
yet still to come.

My Grandmother's name
long past now,
but still Her light carves my mind.
Though I never knew Her
I know Her still.
Though I could not touch Her,
my breast beats beneath Hers.
Reflecting the tremors of Her
heartbeat gone,
yet still lives on in me.

If I knew not Her voice,
powerful sonata to my listening ear,
I hear Her drum beats in my mind's eye.
I feel the rhythms to which She once
moved and still moves today.
I retrace Her footsteps
while entrenching my own.
Together we blend
creating a new path as I
chant my warrior song of life.

A Dedication to Sistahs who lead

You my sistah I look to at all times

You, my sistah I admire, in your prime

When you care for yourself you shine

Oh my sistah, keep feeling fine.

Introduction Part I: Reaffirming Spirit

This book is about Afrikan women, written for the Afrikan nation. By Afrikan women, I mean all of my sistahs, sistahs of Afrikan descent, whether we recently hail from the Dominica Republic, Brazil or England, whether we call ourselves Angela or Akua. Some of us may call ourselves Afrikan American, Black British, or Bajan etc. But no matter what label we use to describe ourselves in the Diaspora, the one thing we all have in common is our roots, our common ancestry. Thus, the purpose of this book is to provide simple lessons in living for the Afrikan nation. In the seventeen chapters contained here, you will find gems for self-development and self-empowerment. Motivational, inspirational chapters which will try to galvanise you to aim for your star. Each chapter begins with a poem which sets the tone for the essay, exploring the essence of spirited Afrikan women.

I strongly believe that Afrikan women are spirited women. When in tune with ourselves, we are indomitable. A confident and spirited Afrikan woman is a joy to behold, for she knows what time it is, and she wants to ensure that she works to make her life and those of her nearest and dearest fulfilled in every sense of the word. A spirited Afrikan woman is not afraid to say what is on her mind, when the times dictate that she does so. A spirited Afrikan woman tries to live and walk truth, even where the speaking of truth is painful to many, including herself. A spirited Afrikan woman is not afraid to analyse herself, and adapt her behaviour when she finds herself wanting. Honour and honesty is the measuring rod by which she defines the worthiness of those in her life, and what better way is there, in these days in which the world is run by people peddling distrust and lies.

The spirited Afrikan woman is not to be messed with, for when she is dealt with in a dishonest manner, her defence mechanisms will come into full force, and she will deal with those who attempt to lower her self-esteem and strength with ruthlessness. Her lines of delineation between right and wrong are simply drawn, and not easily confused. The spirited Afrikan woman thus, lives as a role model for all those in her life, and for the future. Be sure in the knowledge that every Afrikan woman has the potential to live spiritedly. Know also that if we give of ourselves to those in need, without expecting anything in return; if we listen to our inner voices, and refuse to be swayed by a tumultuous world; if we assert our values, when we know that they are the right ones for us; if we determine to stay in the light, when so many around us cling to darkness, then we will live spirited lives, content in the knowledge that the secret of life is simply being. It really is as simple as that; knowing that life exists so that we can be, be whatever we want to be. be it in pain, be it in love, be it in education. When we accept that life is only about existence, and the contribution that we make to this world, it allows us to come to the realisation that obstacles, failures and triumphs are all a necessary part of the circle of life.

Afrikan women who are seeking the strength of spirit can certainly try to enrich their lives by living in the light, and developing themselves as strong role models for their own self-esteem, and for those Afrikan women around the world who find themselves in painful, subjugated situations. Taking the step to develop your character will surely lead to the strengthening of, and an understanding of your spiritual path, thus giving direction to your life.

These lessons in living stand as a challenge to all of us to strive to be the best that we can be, in all things. The messages and lessons that you will find contained within this book are not new. I am sure that much will be familiar to you. Indeed, all of the lessons of this book lie within you, waiting to be affirmed. Thus, this book stands as an anchor by which you may re-affirm, and remind yourself of that which you already know. Or, at the very least it will challenge those of us who are at the beginning of seeking our inner selves, to develop the best within us, not the minimum. In exposing yourself to the concepts of this book with an open mind, you allow yourself the many blessings of a truly spirited existence.

Follow the statements of self-affirmation at the end of each chapter carefully. These statements are tools for change and development. By studying and practising each self-affirmation statement for thirty days, you are assured that their message will stay with you forever, as long as you continue to practise them. Thirty days is recommended because it is well known that it takes at least thirty days to form a new habit; to get the new practice lodged in your mind. If you find thirty days is too difficult to maintain for all sixteen chapters, try practising for thirteen days, for the number thirteen is a magical number, the figure for re-birth. It represents twelve months to a year plus one more for a new year. It represents the transformation of a full moon into a new moon, each month Thus, by studying these chapters for at least thirteen days, you ensure your rebirth into positiveness, not to mention a spirited existence.

Introduction Part II: A Woman's Place

Historically, what has been the Afrikan woman's place? The best way to describe the historical role of the Afrikan woman is to say that it has been diverse. Although there is an exclusive role for women in Afrikan nationhood, that role is not limiting and may be expanded in many directions. The list of our Sheroes, and their contribution to the civilisation of the world, has been so great as to document this. So many of our sistahs' names are not recorded in the annals of history, because their contributions have been discounted. So, in all likelihood, there must be countless more that should be added, perhaps your grandmother, mother or aunt.

So many Afrikan women throughout the world accept the lot, which we believe, has been bequeathed to us. But bequeathed to us by whom? Sometimes to our discredit we do not feel challenged enough to step forward and forge a different destiny for ourselves. Perhaps we too readily believe the perception that Afrikan women do not do things, rather we get things done to us. That is, we are not the 'subject' of any event, actually making things happen, but instead we are the 'object', the thing that gets moved about; the pawn in the chess game. If so this is the wrong perception to hold, for it stops us from achieving, in every sphere of our lives. There are so many things that a woman might want to do in her lifetime, which encompass an entire spectrum of different ideas. But because it is accepted by many that we should only have one profession in our lifetimes, we walk away from the riches that could be ours; spiritual, educational, physical, emotional, professional riches.

Who defines what is acceptable to Afrikan women? Sadly, often times the Afrikan woman does not contribute to the debate of what she wants out of her life. Nor indeed what she wants for her children and her man. This is a problem that only Afrikan women can rectify, by allowing our voices to be heard through the medley of others that clamour for attention. Strong Afrikan women, women who speak out are a blessing not a curse. We bring duality to the male/female relationship. Without us, the view of the man is given preference and is over-emphasised, bringing many problems to the Afrikan family. We need to live up to the legacy of our spirited female ancestors who contributed much to Afrikan technology, spirituality and nationhood.

From Afrika to the Americas, Europe, and Asia we are Afrikan people. We are not simply Black, never coloured, West Indian, Negro, European, American or just an ethnic minority. None of these labels sum up the total that makes us the people that we are today. The name by which we label ourselves is paramount in ensuring our holistic development; for incorrect labels invariably lead to dysfunctional behaviour, poor cultural reference and identity. As Afrikan people we are unique, we move to the rhythm of the inspirational drum as we listen to the messages from our ancestors.

Those Who Came Before

Spirited Afrikan women, sheroes, in the tradition of Saraounia, Queen Sheba, Nehanda, Yaa Asantewaa, Fumilayo Ransome-Kuti, Queen Amina, Claudia Jones, Nanny of the Maroons and Winnie Mandela, to mention but a few. The spirit and determination of these Afrikan women stand as a testament to the power of all of us, that we can achieve and contribute the maximum to ourselves, and to our people.

Afrikan women have much to offer the world. However, reaching our full potential means releasing the negativity, which follows many of us all our lives. Chasing negativity out of our lives can be a painful experience, as it demands letting go of old habits and changing for the better. Many of us may prefer to live with the hurt of bad habits, or negative situations. Yet, by taking steps to see what the mountain is like on the other side opens us up to the many possibilities of life.

Traditionally, Afrikan women have been mothers, lovers, and wives. But we have also been warriors in the best of our tradition, such as Queen Candace, Queen Sheba, Queen Hatshepsut, Harriet Tubman and Josina Machel, some of whom were also leaders of the highest realm in their own right, or alongside their men, such as Queen Tiye and Nefetari. We have been High Priestesses, technologists, farmers, business women etc. There is very little that Afrikan women have not contributed to. Today Afrikan women have fought in wars in places such as Eritrea, Zimbabwe and Namibia; following the path that they desire for their people. Afrikan women are tired of seeing their people butchered and killed in so-called liberation wars, in which Afrikan kills Afrikan. Why do we feel we need to liberate ourselves from each other, just because Europeans defined us a certain way and named Afrika according to their own design? Now many of us accept these descriptions and want to rule the land in a similar way to which the European did during colonisation. In Liberia, in Sierra Leone, in Angola, in Guinea Conakry, Afrikan women are tired of burial rites for our children. We will fight to stop this in the best way that we can; through our own voices and refusal of collusion, but also with our own action where necessary.

Afrikan Renaissance

Afrikan women need to be in solidarity throughout the world, and to give a voice to the dispossessed of our people. Afrika is in the state she is today, not only because of the onslaught from invaders and the corrupt, but also because her daughters have been dissuaded from having a voice in deciding her future. All Afrikan countries are using a model of governance, which disadvantages women and allows us no voice, or at the most a marginal voice. It is now time for sistahs to do it for ourselves and lifting up our children and supporting our men as we proceed. We need to work in unison with Afrikan men, not against them, and reverse the path that Afrika has been forced along in the past thousand or so years. It is important that we do not start to ostracise our men, or even marginalise them as we have allowed ourselves to be marginalised today. What we have to recognise is that Afrika once had a system before slavery holocaust, colonisation and imperialism, which protected men and women and recognised the complimentary roles of both. We need to get back to that system if we are going to move our continent forward and beyond the realms of the neo-colonialist's control. It is now time for us to remove the colonial and neo-colonial stooges of Afrika and replace them with women and men willing and able to serve the people. More than anything today, Afrika needs men and women of the people, for the people. With men and women of the people, the major problems besetting Afrika today would be solved. Poverty and underdevelopment could be smashed and eliminated through work to this end; which in turn comes about through faith in our ability to solve our own problems in our own way.

I believe that while Afrika remains in bondage (mental as well as physical) all of her people, wherever they live, will also remain in bondage. Afrikan people whether living here in England, in France, in Brazil, in Grenada, in the USA or wherever, will continue to be judged by the state of our homeland. Though many of us might attempt to run from our Afrikan connections, the truth is, it is impossible for the tree to cut off its roots without dying. While some might attempt to deny their heritage, other groups of people most definitely identify us all as Afrikans, regardless of where we are born. Therefore, if we want to improve our individual lives, we will most definitely need to improve the lot of Afrika as a continent. Only when Afrika has her respect back can all of her people shout 'free at last' in the fullest sense of the phrase.

Reclaiming Our Space

Afrikan women have a key contribution to make in transforming Afrika from the battered continent that she often is today, into the glorious Queen that she can be. We, Afrikan women cannot leave the leadership of our countries, or our continent solely in the hands of our men folk who, in the main, have frequently shown themselves to have different priorities over the last three decades. The traditional Afrikan system of leadership, which respects the complimentary roles of both men and women, needs to be exploited, in order to right the wrongs in Afrika. Afrikan women are best suited to play a key role in the development of Afrika, because we do not typically allow our egos to blind our minds to the best option in a given situation. We need to use our mediating skills to bring order and balance to Afrika. That is a challenge that only we can answer. It is a challenge long overdue.

Afrikan women are the last bastions of Afrikan culture, because they protect Afrikan culture, which is under attack from culturally deprived peoples. The protection of the foods that we eat is part of the maintenance of Afrikan culture. The seeds that were hidden in our clothing, even as we ourselves were stolen from our homeland, into enslavement in the Caribbean (New Afrikan Islands) and the Americas, are an indication of the perseverance of our culture through diversity. It was through determination and perseverance that we are able to still maintain the culture embodied in our foods. Today, the foods that we eat in the New Afrikan Islands are very similar and some even have the same names as those in Afrika. To us yam is yam, plantain is plantain. Ogi (i.e. boiled corn wrapped in banana leaves) in Nigeria is called pami in Trinidad and Tobago. Thankfully, Afrikan traditions from the Afrikan continent survived the slavery holocaust; and that existence, that survival can be seen in the New Afrikan Islands today. The names that we give to our children, survived. The songs that we sing to our children, survived. The moral stories and fables that we tell around the evening fire, survived. The cultural norms of the Afrikan family lay embodied in the Afrikan woman, and through her they survive and are replenished. As Omowale Malcolm X stated, "The strength of a nation can be determined by the level of education of its women."

The Afrikan woman stands as the vanguard of the Afrikan family. This is a theme, which has been a dominant part of Afrikan women's lives for centuries. We are renown as the strong force that maintains the Afrikan family even under extreme attack. We work hard to ensure that our families survive, if not intact, at least enduring. Many hardships are undergone to allow those we love better lives. We push on through the anger of young adulthood as we come to understand the glass ceiling that is placed above us, blocking our progression. We push on while the many avenues of drug addiction and crime are opened as 'natural' alternatives to us. We push on through the financial hardships of providing for the family and through the broken relationships with our men. Hell, but it isn't always about Afrikan women heading one-parent families! Even where the Afrikan man and woman remain together there are many challenges and obstacles that we face together. The financial problems are still there, the social pressures of crime are still there, the mis-education of the

Afrikan child is still there. But again the Afrikan woman plays a central role in maintaining the family. Compromising to reach that necessary consensus or, typically, as the voice of reason, the Afrikan woman is there.

Afrikan women have traditionally been thought of as the centre of the social system that existed and exists throughout Afrika . Our systems of rule and governance in many Afrikan countries were very much dependent on consultation between the ruler (who would often be the King) with the elder Queen mother, as well as consultation with the elders of the community. Each person had a voice and had a right to be satisfied by the ruler. Indeed, in the Ashantene system of governance, a person had the right to stay before the King or Queen until he or she was completely satisfied that the leader had responded adequately to his or her needs. Afrikan art frequently glorifies the special place of Afrikan women. A few Afrikan societies have even been created around the reverence of the symbol of female genitalia, that is, Afrikan womanhood. A case in point would be the Great Wall of Zimbabwe, built by the Shona people around 1100CE (Christian or Common Era).

Historically, the Afrikan woman's place has been any place she wants it to be. For she alone is unique in defining her own space, when she is on top of the world.

Thank-you Mama

I wanna thank-you Mama
I wanna thank-you Mama for every -
thing that you have done for me.
I wanna thank-you Mama for being so
strong
I wanna thank-you Mama for keeping
me oh so long
for bearing me
for loving me
cherishing me
teaching me
clothing me
suckling me
touching me
feeding me
seeking me
scolding me
paining for me
fearing for me
praying for me
wishing for me
bequeathing to me
I wanna thank-you Mama for everything
that you have done for me

Thank you Maria

Thank You Mama

Afrikan women have long been hailed as true mothers of the earth, nurturing their children and, indeed, other peoples' children with hardly a breath for themselves. Afrikan woman have experienced a history of great hardship in the last five hundred years. The stories of the Afrikan Mama in the Americas, in the New Afrikan Islands (the Caribbean), and indeed in Afrika itself, are many. There are the Afrikan women who were used as mothers to white children during the Afrikan slavery holocaust ordeal. Afrikan women had their own children snatched from their breasts while white children were put to suckle there instead. Afrikan women who suffocated their children, rather than see them live on in a life of slavery and oppression. Afrikan women forced to breed with a variety of different men, more than likely all of them not of their choice. Up to every six months after having given birth to a child, Afrikan women would be bred again. Their children, the product of these many unions, were then sold into different slaveholding families as soon as they could stand on their own feet.

Afrikan women were beaten while heavily pregnant until their backs ran a river of red. Afrikan pregnant women had their stomachs slit, their foetuses ripped out and trodden into the earth while they screamed in agony, were left to bleed to death. This was often done just in order to strike terror into the minds and hearts of all Afrikans who observed. It was believed that these Afrikan observers, who were unwilling witnesses to these acts of genocide, would then fully understand the unrelenting wickedness of the European slave-master and

3

would not rebel against him. (This belief was, of course, misplaced). Afrikan women raped and derogated by the white slave-master, while their husbands were in the same room feeling powerless to intercede and defend them; then beaten by the white mistress because the master had laid with them. Afrikan women working the field, up to sixteen hours a day, while heavily pregnant, even giving birth to their children in the very field where they laboured. Afrikan women hung for speaking back to a white man or a white woman. Afrikan women maimed for daring to further themselves by reading and writing. Afrikan women afraid for their children and their men.

Afrikan women forced to work as the servants of whites and others even after emancipation day and up 'til today. Afrikan women in domesticated service throughout European industry, the early morning cleaners, and late evening slavers for small money, working for petty minded people. Afrikan women forced to defend their children against the negative impact of stereotypes within the school system, often times without the benefit and comfort of the Afrikan man by her side. Afrikan women forced to defend her children against racist police forces within her neighbourhood. Afrikan women going without to ensure that their children, and even their men have a chance for greater things in the future, be it an education or a profession or even a material item, or a piece of food. Afrikan women sacrifice the world over. Through all these trials and tribulations, the Afrikan woman has survived and triumphed, because she can.

The Afrikan woman stands as an inspiration to her children, both male and female. She is a living role model. As Afrikan women we are at our best when we have had the positive influence of education, then we are able to teach our children through a positive influence of the old with the new, a clever synthesis of the traditional with the modern. The Afrikan woman and mother is the first role model for her child. Even as the child gestates within her womb, the mother teaches her unborn child, through her responses to stimuli from the surrounding environment. By her temperament, the Afrikan mother is able to pass on emotions and temperament to the unborn child, an important starting point for all children, and not to be underestimated. Even more importantly, once the child is born, it is usually the mother who acts as the first point of reference for the newly born child. It is usually the mother who responds to the child's every need and teaches the child about the world. Therefore, it is hardly surprising that the Afrikan mother's strength is an important characteristic that can be acquired by the child through learning from this important role model.

Well-rounded and grounded people are normally so, because of the positive relationship they have developed, with their mothers in the first instance, and the rest of the family circle. Specifically, the spirited Afrikan woman often learns her moral and spiritual beliefs from her mother. She tries to maintain a warm and loving relationship with her parents, especially her mother, whom she identifies as the centre of her moral learning. Through the positive relationship she maintains with her parents she is able to move on to warm and caring relationships with those she later comes into contact with. On the other hand, dysfunctional people tend to be dysfunctional because of their poor social relationships, which often include an initial poor relationship with their mothers. Mothers should be the epitome of what is important in a person's life. It is the mother who is the nurturer of all life on this earth. Indeed it is mother earth that gives us all life. Hence, respect is due. Fortunately, today, Afrikans in the Diaspora, let alone Afrika proper, have not lost their reverence for the mother image. Even within Diaspora Afrikan cultures, which have experienced terrible changes, due to a legacy of oppression, such as in America, Afrikans still understand that to disrespect a person's mother, is to disrespect the essence of that person. That reverence we can be grateful for; for it is at least an indication that Afrikan cultural norms are still present within the Diaspora, even though they undoubtedly need strengthening.

Afrikan mothers need to be recognised for their contribution to civilisation and nationhood; Afrikan mothers who have struggled to give a better life to their children, a life free of poverty, a life with choices and possibilities. The Afrikan woman is the comforter and the director for many. Her love is so strong, she is never certain of where she will end up, all through the love of her child.

Recognise that
- The Mother principle is one of the most important symbols in Afrikan nationhood and must be nurtured and protected within our communities.
- The power embodied within our Mothers will only be *fully* harnessed in an environment, which respects the role of the Father principle, encouraging duality.

Self-affirmation
- I nurture the mother principle within me.
- I nurture the father principle within me.
- I encourage duality between the roles of father and mother in my family, community and nation.
- I respect mothers and fathers within my family circle and community.
- I encourage young people within my family circle and community to respect our mothers and fathers.

Smiles Within

You are beautiful to me

You are beautiful
because
you are more than one

You are beautiful to me
You are beautiful
because
your eyes smile
beautiful rays of warm ebony
chocolate pools of sunshine
bathing my sight so I cry

You are beautiful
to me
your expressions
tender reflections
of a loving spirit
you cannot hide
nor should you want to

You are beautiful
to me
your voice echoes
calming, shivering ripples
of depths un-searched
that touch my spine
in a tingling
search
for
my
inner
deeper
womanhood
You are beautiful to me

Natural Soul-Mates

The Afrikan man should be the most important person in any Afrikan woman's life. He is her natural partner and mate. He should be her support and back up during the good times and the bad. The relationship between the Afrikan man and woman should be one of duality and complimentary. If that relationship does not exist for you, it's time to create it.

Afrikan men are beautiful, they have the capacity to share so much with Afrikan women. We must do much to maintain a spirit of love and sharing in our relationships. By sharing our deepest fears and successes with our men, we open ourselves up to a whole host of new possibilities.

Admittedly, relationships are fraught with problems. However, these are not insurmountable, and can be dealt with through honesty and understanding. Yet, no amount of honesty or understanding will be enough if you enter a love-relationship when you are not ready for it. The worst possible thing any Afrikan woman can do is to enter into a relationship when she is not ready for the demands and challenges that it entails. Fear of what others want us to do, or think, should not be a determining factor in our decision. An Afrikan woman can never afford to get involved in a sex relationship when she does not know the man she is letting into her bed. Time must be taken to understand what we want and what our prospective partner wants out of life, before we jump into each other's bed. Actions taken without an understanding of who we are and who the men in our lives are only lead to confusion and ultimately the destruction of the relationship before it has even taken off the ground; simply because we don't really understand what the other person is looking for in us. Love relationships should only be entered into when we are totally ready to ensure that we bring the best of ourselves to the union, with some level of certainty of its survival. The best thing an Afrikan woman can be with her prospective lover is a friend first, for the respect formed during friendship will act as an anchor in the forthcoming love relationship.

The positive qualities of the Afrikan man are not hard to find, contrary to a lot of the bad mouthing that is circulating the globe about our men folk. Bad mouthing that we as Afrikan women contribute to and perpetuate. Nowadays if you do not bad mouth your Afrikan man, either something is wrong with you or something is dreadfully wrong with him. For, aren't Afrikan men supposed to be 'worthless,' 'good-for-nothing,' 'lazy,' 'three-timing scoundrels?' Wrong! Afrikan men are many things including industrious, hard-working, loving, dedicated, and sharing, as well as powerful role models for our children. As Afrikan women, it is wrong for us to spread malicious stereotypes on the basis of our bad, or even not so bad experiences with Afrikan men. Some Afrikan men might have a majority of negative behaviours, while others may have few. Afrikan men are most definitely not born with a host of negative habits, but circumstance undoubtedly contributes to the way in which some of our men turn out. Every Afrikan man will be unique, and it is wrong to place our brothas all at the same juncture in life. As Afrikan women we have to come to an understanding of why some of our men behave in the way that they do, and try to assist them to grow better. Certainly it will be difficult to do this, without having an understanding of the various obstacles Afrikan people face in life and even more poignantly, recognition of the history of Afrikan peoples over the past two thousand years.

The qualities to search for in the Afrikan man should be the qualities that you would like for yourself. If you cannot see them in the prospective Afrikan man in your life, it is time to go to work and nurture them together. Few Afrikan men are going to hold all of the attributes that you deem as important, just as

10

you yourself will not hold all the attributes you perceive to be important in life. But the most important thing is that you help your man to be the best that he can be with patience and dedication. Ultimately, we must realise that love is not about fixing or changing your man. We should avoid acting as mechanics, ready to replace what we view as a defunct attribute within our men, with a spare part. Sadly, often times in our desire for love we search for a mythical unique man and leave ourselves open to abuses by men unworthy of our attention; simply because we are willing to try all manner of men who are incompatible with ourselves. We can waste a lot of energy on developing a role for the Afrikan men in our lives, which they do not want for themselves. Afrikan men should not be pushed into arenas that they are uncomfortable with, simply because we deem those arenas to be important. Afrikan women do not have the authoritative voice on what is right for Afrikan men. We can only contribute to their development, not dictate it to them. This contribution will only come through increased communication between man and woman.

Of course our men must be challenged to reach for the heights and to achieve the best that they can. They must be encouraged to be creative in their endeavours, to seek viable livelihoods for themselves and their families, and not to overly rely on employment from those uninterested in our welfare. And who better to urge our men to reach these heights than the Afrikan woman?

Sadly, Afrikan women are often searching for Afrikan men in all manner of unsuitable places, hoping that the He of our dreams is waiting for us to come along. However, we may just have to accept that the He of our dreams is not in that place, nor is he likely to be. Finding the Afrikan man who is going to be a true love-mate in these times may necessitate that we look in some previously inconceivable places, places that do not readily or easily come to mind. Perhaps a long time friend who has always been a comforter, a mail man, a carpenter, a plumber, in fact any manner of workers or not workers as the case may be. For, if we as Afrikan women define our desire for

Afrikan men on the basis of their ability to maintain a job, we are opening ourselves up to a whole host of problems. And not any job at that, but a job that meets our high standards of deemed 'professionalism,' or quality of job, which meets some media definition of power-packing jobs. So the man who works with his hands as a builder or plumber might be devalued in our concept of what an Afrikan man should be. This is not only wrong, but also extremely dangerous in these times of large-scale rejection of Afrikan males as employable people by western industry.

What kind of situation are we breeding for our nation if we are going to define our men only in the context of whether they are employed or not? Afrikan women need to get real and understand the situation in which we find ourselves as Afrikan people. We should not contribute to the devaluation of our men by stating that they are worthless simply because they cannot find a job in western industry. This is not to state that we should tolerate laziness within our homes, for our men can contribute to the daily maintenance of our homes, rather than sit back, relax and expect the Afrikan woman to return from work and deal with housework and childcare, after the unemployed man has been doing very little with his day. As Afrikan women we cannot support that kind of situation, but we can aide our men to develop more creative roles for themselves, especially in these days in which they have to deal with economic rejection.

Often times Afrikan men may view what you did as a single woman as acceptable to attract him. But subsequently, after your commitment to him and vice versa, pressure may be brought from his side for you to change your activities or behaviour, which is deemed no longer acceptable. This might require changing the sports you do, the clothes you wear, the job you have, the car you drive, etc. These kinds of demands, based on male pre-conceptions of what an attached woman should be, are not acceptable. Afrikan women have to fight hard not to bend to the will of our men on those petty issues. It is necessary to stand firm, for where will you eventually draw the line on your right to make your own decisions. Afrikan men must be willing to listen to the voices of Afrikan women, without feeling threatened, taking on board her suggestions and aspirations and aiding her to achieve them. It is an increasingly rare Afrikan man who can listen to his woman in a spirit of equality. In cases where Afrikan men find it difficult to respect our free choice, we must demand it.

Expectations in a relationship are an important concept to understand. We all have expectations of the people in our lives. If they are a friend, we may expect them to listen to us, to support us through our triumphs and failures, to offer advice, to spend time with us. If they are our family, we may expect them to put up with our foul moods and to always support us no matter what we do. If they are our love-mate, we may expect them to comfort us, to support us, to love us and develop with us. The list of expectations in relationships may be endless.

The funny thing about expectations is that most of the time they live within the domain of the mind. Sometimes the expectations may seem obvious, because they are socially defined and acceptable to the culture, for example, the expectation that a mother nurtures her child. However, within a love relationship, expectations are not always verbally declared between man and woman; they are simply sent through non-verbal cues. The trouble with non-verbal cues is that not everybody is good at decoding them and not everybody is good at sending them in the first place. This may result in problems within a love-relationship. For you might have an expectation of your man that he is not clear on, and vice versa. Then when either one of you consistently fail to live up to those expectations, maybe simply because you did not know, tensions and problems will build up. Often times this problem occurs because sistahs are not always good at expressing themselves in a relationship or brothas aren't. Or you both failed to define some of your basic expectations at the start of your relationship. In which case you will need to start to talk and reach an understanding of your expectations of each other. There is nothing wrong with making demands of each other. What is wrong is making demands of somebody and not letting them know about the demands, and then being angry with that person for letting you down. When, in all honesty, they may have let you down because they simply did not know. Sometimes we may not want to voice our expectations because it seems needy, as if we are cramping somebody's style, and because we have to reveal ourselves, which makes us feel vulnerable. Well, rightly so. Being in a relationship is about making some necessary demands and it is about showing the real you. You are together with your love-mate because you want something from that person and you want to give something to that person. Therefore you will need to make some demands and yes, voice some expectations.

Afrikan woman, don't be afraid to let your feelings be known. Afrikan women and man are sadly becoming notorious for the inability to express their expectations of each other, and then becoming mad when we feel we have been let down. Talk, communicate and express your expectations and these problems will become few and far between.

Recognise that
- At all times we must know that if we love and respect ourselves, we will attract men who love and respect us also. However, if we hate and despise ourselves, we will attract men who will hate and despise us too. Make sure that you love who you are, before you expect another hue-man being to love you too.
- A revolutionary spirited Afrikan woman cannot have a reactionary man in her life. This would be a mix doomed for failure. A revolutionary woman should not have to bend to the qualms of a man with lesser ideals. Any movement to do so will only lead to her stagnation, and hurt on both sides.
- A relationship should be based on trust, friendship and love, for longevity.
- No Afrikan man is perfect; therefore do not unconstructively put him down, because of his faults.

14

- You can stand with your man or against him, through your actions or inaction.
- A man cannot be measured by the job that he does or does not have, nor by the money he does or does not earn, but rather by the essence of who he is.
- Love is given unconditionally.

Self-affirmation
- I have the qualities that I need to make my love-relationship work with my natural soul mate.
- I am loving and understanding of my man and encourage him to be the best that he can be.
- I am not afraid to speak my mind when I believe it is in the best interests of my man and my family.
- I support my man, just as I expect him to support me.
- I always express my expectations of my man in order to aide our communication.
- I do not want a baby for a man who is going to hide behind my apron. But rather, a man who is going to stand up as a role model for me and for our children, even as I stand as a role model for him.
- Afrikan man, I do not need you to wash my clothes, cook my food, give me gifts or take me places. I just want you to love and respect me, as I love and respect you in return. But if loving me means that you feel you want to wash my clothes, cook my food, give me gifts and take me places, I will give thanks for your generosity.

Sistahs

Sistahs keep you on track
Sistahs never look back
Sistahs make you feel fine
Sistahs together define and defy time

Sistahs share their love
Sistahs make you laugh
Sistahs pave the way
each and every day

Sistahs never give up
Sistahs keep you on top
istahs back you up
'till they overfill your cup

Sistahs make you shine
Sistahs together cry
Sistahs prepare your mind
Sistahs are so very kind

Sistahs raise your child
Sistahs nurture and love
Sistahs fight for their rights
with all their might

Oh my sistah, keep on, just shine!

Sistahood is Global

Sistahs have to help each other up, raise as we climb, in the tradition of each one teach one. As Afrikan women we can solve many of our problems together by helping each other, listening to each other, or sharing some of the many tasks that we have to complete each day. In much the same way as sistahs share their different chores in agricultural villages, we can do the same, whether we are in a city or not. We can share with our sistahs across the seas not in a patronising manner, but in a progressive manner, to help their lives to be more fruitful.

Often we let pettiness come between us, small issues are blown into bigger issues of conflict and dislike. We have to recognise that we all have our bad days, days when we may feel low, ugly, and unintelligent; money problems may be holding us down, or we allow them to keep us down. But with a little love from those nearest and dearest we are able to overcome these small issues. There are ways in which we can be proactive and inspire others to be the same. Afrikan women are, after all, the best role models for fellow sistahs. We spirited women can pass on our experiences of assertiveness, to push forward the issues that are important to Afrikan women and the Afrikan family in general.

Sometimes when we have gifts, special skills that we have managed to develop, we can be selfish and not share what we know with those that have less. Why is there sometimes an unwillingness to share? Perhaps we feel our skills are for us alone, or we deserve payment before we share them with our sistahs. Our skills may indeed be special, but it does not follow that they are not to be shared. There is something very special about sharing knowledge with those willing to learn. We can inspire our sistahs to seek those things that she might have previously thought were unattainable to her and in so doing, aide her in her self-development.

It may be surprising, but assertiveness is something that the Afrikan woman tends to need, and which some of us sorely lack. Despite the stereotype that Afrikan women are aggressive and thus, one would believe, assertive, many Afrikan women suffer from an absence of assertiveness. Many Afrikan women do not know how to say no, whether it is caring for the sick in our families, to the extent that we put our own health at risk, to the maintenance and financial support of our families, because others who might assume those responsibilities fail to do so. We must know of examples in which a female within the family is left to care for a sick or incontinent or financially insolvent parent, while our brothas often stay in the background and may contribute little in terms of personal care and sometimes finance. Many of us might enjoy the opportunity of caring for a loved one, but some of us may not want to contribute as much as we do, but our strong sense of duty compels us. Even where we make our contribution, it is important to make room for others to take responsibility. We might be surprised to realise that brothas and sistahs may be ready to contribute, but because we are always ready with our time and resources, they hold back and do not come forward.

It is important that we are able to say no to certain situations and not feel guilty about it, or give ourselves hang-ups. We should not feel that we need to justify our positions. You may feel that you do not want to do something, because it simply does not feel right for you, due to any number of reasons. It does not follow that because we say no, we do not care. But it can mean that we may be creating space in which we may be able to manoeuvre a better outcome for ourselves, which might include a more equitable sharing of responsibilities amongst the entire family.

Childcare is a major issue for Afrikan women. The lack of adequate support which may spring from family circumstances, or even from inadequate provision of childcare facilities in our localities, means it is a problem. Whatever the reason, it is usually sistahs who end up solving the problem for each other, by sharing childcare responsibilities. The picking up of each others children from school, looking after them in the home while one sistah parent is working late is one way in which we are able to overcome these challenges. We back each other up because often times we are all we have and there is no alternative. This is not an ideal situation, as it is comparable to two cripples supporting each other through their mutual hardships. Yet, in a world of many difficulties surrounding this particular issue of childcare support, each other is often times all we have.

Sistahs in support of each other is a wonderful thing to behold. The sharing of experiences and knowledge to uplift each other is inspiring. We have to make sure that we keep away from tendencies to hold each other back, in the hope that by blocking our sistah, we might progress further. Nobody truly experiences progress by holding back another. Progress is elusive in these circumstances because the negativity of stepping on another person eventually catches up with us in the most unexpected of places.

In the Diaspora, there is an alarming tendency for young Afrikan women to stare each other out, looking for something to bitch against each other about, looking for a fight or power struggle, looking to make a name, or just looking to kill the boredom, or to catch a man by our rudeness. However, any man that a woman gains due to her winning a fight with her sistah or mother, is not worth having. For his attraction to you will be based on your destructive behaviour, which is not something to be admired or sought after, but something to be avoided. Unfortunately there is a lot of this going on in our communities. The saying is true, that love-relationships may come and go, but friendships last forever. That is why it is important to maintain your friendships through the hard times and to make sure that the love-ship you have was firstly founded on friendship. In this way its chances of survival are increased.

It would appear that these grave tendencies to fight each other over jobs, recognition, money, etc. are formed from the unfortunate fact that those at the bottom of the pile fight each other to make a name. There is a glass ceiling on the progression of Afrikans throughout the world, and you either have to take the firm decision to break that ceiling and rise to the sky, or you will be left fighting with your own brotha and sistah, within the confines that have been created for you by the ruling forces of the world. We are witnessing scenes such as these being played out in our communities when we watch our young Afrikan men and women willing to kill each other for mere progression, or worst still, for sport.

Sometimes we may be tempted to leave our sistahhoods behind when we find something that we consider more fanciful, or pleasant. These sistahhoods that we give up are the very same ones that sustained us through our difficult times. This may be one of the very worst things that we can do within our sistahhood, to disregard a sistah for a new man, a new job, or new hobby. When those of us who come to our senses go back in search of our sistahs, we may find them gone or no longer attainable to us. It takes a very rounded and mature sistah to accept back her whimsical friend, when previously that same friend dropped her like a hot brick.

We may determine that it is in our best interests to keep caring for our testy sistahs from a distance. It is not always possible to maintain friendships in close association with our sistah-friends. It may be that painful inclinations of our sistah-friends are so destructive that they threaten to pull us into the mire with them. If that is the case and we have tried our best to help bring our sistah-friend out of her predicament, to no avail, the next best thing that we can do is to step aside and allow our sistah-friend to learn her own lessons, without our interference. In some circumstances we may determine to stick around, to be there for our sistah-friend when she surfaces, but in other circumstances we may determine that for the sake of our own wholeness and peace of mind, we have to take the difficult step of stating loud and clear 'I'm outta here!'

Sistahs are a powerful force. We are an anchor for each other. If you are lucky enough to develop a timeless friendship with a sistah, you will understand the feeling of being truly blessed. The kind of relationship where you may express yourself honestly, knowing that your voice will be listened to, without any double meaning. These are the kind of sistahhoods that we need to develop. Sistahhoods within which we can learn from each other, from each others mistakes and definitely from our triumphs. We can learn from the wisdom of our elder sistahs, and be inspired the youthful optimism of our younger sistahs.

Recognise that

- Sometimes I do not support my Afrikan sistah the way I ought to, especially where I am tied up with my own problems.
- Sometimes it can be difficult to maintain that feeling of sistahhood through the hardships and set-backs of friendships. But the spirit of oneness can prevail, even in the most difficult of times.
- My sistah deserves my respect and loyalty.
- My sistah is a source of knowledge and power.
- You can increase your own knowledge and capabilities by sharing what you know with your sistah.
- My sistah is not my rival.
- Sistahhoods need to be worked on, they do not function by accident or providence, for what you put in you will get out.
- You must fight to maintain your sistah-friendships, even through the setbacks.
- Both you and your sistah have demanding issues facing you, therefore, try to be understanding of her problems and moods, just as she is of yours.

Self-affirmation

- I have an open mind to the teachings I can learn from my sistah.
- I share all that I can with my sistah.
- I act as my sistah's keeper. I am her balance in times of trouble.
- I love my sistah, just as I love myself.
- I never forsake my sistah.

My Afrikan Child

She smiles, my Afrikan child
A little darling, cuddly, brown,
tender, vulnerable
I guard her.

She is cute, my Afrikan child
mischievous, funny, intelligent,
sharing, creative
I encourage her
to grow

My Afrikan child I will always
nurture you
Help you to learn from your
mistakes
Show you the well of life
though I cannot
and would not
force you
to drink.

My Afrikan child I will always
guide you
cherish you
protect you

How I love you
my beautiful Afrikan child.

A Reaction to fear: Black Boys

To me it seemed a travesty
to carry for so long
nurturing so strong
a seed of beauty.
Only to feel him destroyed
or worst still scared of watching
him die before adulthood

Chapter 5

Nurturing the Afrikan Child

The Afrikan child is a very special child and therefore requires the best from both her parents. Afrikan women should be committed in giving love and attention to the child. The Afrikan mother is the first real reference point to the Afrikan child. It is the mother who carries the child in her womb, nurturing, protecting and responding to the needs of the child. It is the mother who speaks with her child while the child lays gestating in the womb. It is the mother's steady heart beat that comforts the child throughout its incubation period.

Nurturing the Afrikan child will require understanding that the child comes first. The needs of the child must take precedence over the needs of the parents. This should not cause a problem since the needs of the parents and the child will usually not be mutually exclusive. It must be acknowledged that the child is defenceless and requires the support of its parents, in order to make the best choices that will ensure that he or she grows to be a wholesome and well-balanced hue-man being. This will necessitate acknowledging what the child needs to develop a wholesome personality that enjoys life-sustaining experiences. A mother's best gift to her child is to provide an environment in which the child has the opportunity to find herself and to pursue her own interests.

Parents have to make choices that will be to the long-term advantage of the child. Even when it seems that the child might have preferences for other things, parents must decide what necessities for a child are and what are largely inconsequential. Therefore, a good wholesome diet, plenty of

27

fresh air and fresh vegetables and fruits, and clean water are necessities for a strong and healthy body. A challenging intellectual environment which allows a child to explore her mind, coupled with the opportunity to play and learn is necessary for developing a wholesome personality. Unfortunately, not all Afrikan parents throughout the world are able to enjoy giving their child these things. But for those of us who can, this is a must. In particular, mental stimulation which encourages an inquiring mind, and not one that mutely accepts everything, is important; as is a strong moral code, based upon Afrikan cultural norms and practices that are positive for the development of both girls and boys. This means using those Afrikan traditions which are positive and not just using traditions for traditions sake, regardless of whether they are going to pull girls and boys down, and essentially the entire Afrikan culture.

Afrikan children need a historical reference point which establishes for them who they are, where they come from, and who they have the potential to be. Thus, Afrikan children need to be told where they come from, whether they live in Afrika or in the Diaspora. They need a historical perspective on themselves and ultimately all Afrikan people. They need to be told the importance of, and understand their connection to, certain facts and symbols in the world, in language they can comprehend. The importance of education, of self-sufficiency, of doing for self, of critical thinking, etc. is crucial in developing a wholesome character. Many of these factors will be best taught through practical tasks and chores that the child has to carry out on a regular basis, some of which they should receive payment for. In this way we are ingendering an understanding of the importance of reliability, responsibility and reciprocity. At the same time it is important that the Afrikan child does not come to rely on paid work in adulthood, leading to the prevalent problem Afrikan communities in the Diaspora and Afrika experience of paid employment being the norm, rather than creative entrepreneurship, which we need more of.

Afrikan women usually recognise that a child is a child for life. Unfortunately, in the Diaspora, there has been a historical trend of some groups of Afrikan men failing to recognise this fact. We could go into details, historical reasons why this dysfunctional tendency has arisen, but this would not be purposeful at this time. Suffice to say that this fact acts as a lesion within the Afrikan family and needs to be eradicated. Almost hand in hand with this trend has been the tendency to use the Afrikan child as a pawn in disputes between mother and father. Especially where usually the father has finished his relationship with the mother of his child and has a new woman in his life. Then the mother of his child can sometimes make unprecedented demands, perhaps for honest reasons, or perhaps due to her bitterness at the failure of her relationship. This might entail making demands that she knows the father has little chance of fulfilling. When the father subsequently fails to fulfil her demands, some mothers cut off access to the child. Where the father has other children with another woman this situation is often exacerbated, leading to cases in which the child of one mother does not know the children of the other mother. A poor situation indeed, for this, firstly, teaches all children a bad sense of family norms, because of the tension within the family and lack of access to the father. Secondly, it can lead to situations in which, as adults, the brothas and sistahs of the same father may form a love relationship, not realising their sibling connection. An uncommon but not impossible outcome.

Afrikan children are not pawns to be dallied around by parents interested in getting revenge. Mothers of children with the same father must work together to give their children a sense of family-hood. They must not cause the children to suffer from undue tension by creating power struggles or bitching about the other woman and the other children. Once a child has been created, regardless of its parentage, that child deserves proper nurturing. It would be very special if siblings of the same father, but different mother, or vice versa, could recognise each other as blood, as if they were of the same parents. As Afrikan women we must look upon all Afrikan children that we know as our daughters and sons and act accordingly. We must do this regardless of whether we had a relationship with the child's father in the past.

Recognise that
- If you are not mentally whole as a person, you cannot be whole as a parent, and you in turn set your child off at a disadvantage. For your child will develop better if she experiences positive situations in her early years.
- A child requires nurturing first and foremost.
- Children need space to grow. Young adults need room to make their own choices and learn from their own mistakes.
- Children are not pawns to be misused for our own personal gain.
- Children need parental discipline at an early stage in their lives, in order to have self-discipline in adulthood.
- Children require boundaries and moral teachings to assist them in their choices.
- Children require parents before they require friends, in order to develop. The aim of parenthood is not for your child to always like what you tell them. There is nothing wrong with saying no to your child.

Self-affirmation
- I am always a parent to my child.
- I provide my child with discipline.
- I do not use my child as a pawn in any game.
- I provide my child, as a young adult with choices.
- I provide a caring, loving and encouraging environment, seeking to help my child to develop her full potential.

Love

I want time to love

and time to love me.

Love Yourself

Be a well woman all of your life and love yourself as only you can. To maintain wholesome and meaningful relationships in your life, love yourself with all your might. Take the time Afrikan woman to show yourself that you care for your life, for it is precious.

Take time to do the things that you enjoy and love. Take time to be with the people that you love and who love you. Develop a support system of people who believe in you and who love you. You need honest people around you, who will tell you when you are doing right, when you are doing wrong, and make suggestions as to how they can assist you in developing your full potential.

Take time to catch up on the "I've always wanted to" before it's too late. You do have the right to fulfil your own dreams. Do not put your aspirations on hold for lack of time, because for so many of us, tomorrow will never come. Seize the time and make your life count.

Remember that although you are a perfect representation of the Creator's creative force on earth, you are not perfect as a hue-man being, none of us are. The beauty in life is striving to make the inner self as perfect as it can be, without demanding that we change our God-given structures, our body temples and a fully formed soul. Remember, we make mistakes not because we want to, but because they are a part of life's lessons to all of us. The art is not to be harsh on ourselves, but to accept our mistakes as a hue-man failing and use them as building blocks for a better future. Welcome the many qualities that you possess, and use each one of those to your own advantage.

For the blessings of your family, give thanks each and everyday, remembering that each of our lives is short in the total span of creation. Therefore, we should take each opportunity to enjoy our families. We should nurture the relationships that we have within the family and try not to take them for granted.

Take control of the stresses that you experience in your life. Do not allow them to get out of control. But, rather channel the minimum stresses that you feel, so that they work for you, not against you. The major stresses that you face must be squashed before they can take effect on your health. One of the major crises which will face Afrikan women in the 21st century is the battle to maintain our health. Some Afrikan women delight in managing their lives as if they were permanently in a trauma centre. Some Afrikan women have limited choices and are forced to live their lives in that fashion. But it is by no means an ideal situation. It is likely that during the 21st century Afrikan women will continue to suffer a higher than average incidence of fibroids, hypertension and high blood pressure, etc., which are all in some way correlated with stress. One of the most effective ways to prevent these illnesses is to manage stress appropriately so that it does not debilitate us.

Recognise that

- You should make the moment that you are living in as full as you can, for all life is precious.
- You need to take time to explore the inner you; to answer those questions about yourself that are not readily available, for you are a complex person.
- Love yourself for who you are, not for who you want to be. As you develop yourself into who you want to be, you will also love the new you.
- Love yourself by respecting yourself. Do not allow others to take advantage of you, just so that they might fulfil their own end. Recognise your full worth. Challenge all those

who see you as a stepping stone, rather than a hue-man being with aspirations.

- Develop your ability to say NO, firmly and directly. Encourage your own assertiveness. Practise your own assertiveness. Recognise that you are your own best anchor and support system. If you cannot or will not support yourself, few other people will have the time, energy or the love to do it on your behalf. Nor should they. It is your responsibility to demonstrate the care you have for yourself, by doing it for yourself. Help yourself to grow by asking questions and seeking the right answers.
- You can ensure longevity by loving yourself.
- You have the right to do what you want with your life, to develop yourself as only you can.
- You need time in order to achieve.
- You are best served by surrounding yourself with positive people.

Self-affirmation
- I keep balance within my life.
- I love myself first and foremost.
- I protect my life by avoiding stress and unnecessary risks.
- I have a supportive circle of people, who love and believe in me.
- I do not entertain negativity within my mind, nor associate with negative people.

Choices

I have choices
You have choices
She has choices
We have choices
Choices to go here
Choices to go there
Choices to do this
Choices to do that
Choices that say go
Choices that say stay

I have choices
You have choices
She has choices
We have choices
Choices that say **be** strong
Choices that say live weak
Choices that say shout back
Choices that say be meek
Choices that say do for self
Choices that say beg for help

I have choices

You have choices

She has choices

We have choices

Sistahs let's make our own choices.

Second Choice is no Choice

The first thing that you as an Afrikan woman want in life is the best thing for you to attain. This is as true of whether you are looking to choose yourself a reliable, responsive and loving man in your life, as it is for your professional and educational choices. Afrikan women all over the world give up their desires for the sake of their man, their child, their mother, their father, their sick relative, their friend, their fear, or even for the sake of peace. But there might be an alternative way to you assisting those in your life, without giving up your right to choose your lifestyle. We need to explore these alternatives before we give in to the whims of others, however genuine. Our desires are just as important as anybody else's.

Always keep in mind what your number one desire is and work on it until you achieve it. When number one has been attained, then move on to number two and so on. In this methodical way everything that you want in life can be yours. But you have to identify your options and make your own choices first.

If one wants to be a doctor, why settle for a receptionist? Let not the cost, the hard work or other peoples' disbelief stop you from choosing the good that is accessible to you. If you want to run your own business rather than rely on somebody else for employment, then why stop trying to achieve your goal? You have every reason to try and indeed succeed.

Often times we live our lives in other people's image; willing to remain true to somebody else's expectations or dreams. The other person might be a parent, a friend or the man in your life. But regardless of who it is, it is incorrect. You must live your life according to your own ideals and a belief, focusing on what you believe is right and good for you. Make the right choices for you at all times, and do not allow somebody else to make those choices on your behalf.

So many young Afrikan people are living in despair, through lack of opportunities, lack of choice. Yet it becomes so easy for those of us who have choices to take them for granted and not utilise them properly. But everyday, those of us that have choices should realise the unique opportunity that we have to make a contribution. In a world in which many people are struggling to put their daily bread into their mouths, you should give thanks that you have options. Give thanks that you have access to leisure time in which you may read and philosophise, time to enrich your life through books, gaining knowledge that you should put to good use.

Many Afrikan women fall for the second choice option because others are convinced that they cannot make it. Making it is not the most important thing in life. It is satisfying to be accomplished, but in the words of Booker T Washington, 'a person is to be measured not so much by where he has reached in life, but by the obstacles that he has overcome to achieve his aims.'

How is it possible to measure the choices of Mackala who, living in a poor village on one of the New Afrikan Islands, fights to start the first free legal advice service for the dispossessed in her country; with that of Sibongile, raised in France, daughter of a land-owning family, who enters law school and later sets up her own private law practice. It is impossible to compare the two lives, indeed they should not be compared; both women having followed their first choice and succeeded, but from what different circumstances.

We should not choose our professions, loves, or friendships based on fear of them failing, and thereby turn to the second option. We should not choose our professions, loves and friendships based on what our parents want for us, but on what we want for ourselves, on our heartfelt desires. What thoughts cause us to be galvanised first thing in the morning. Is it raising our voice in song, is it sitting down to paint that timeless piece of art or is it dancing, dancing, dancing, dancing. Whatever we feel, we should be doing in our hearts. This is our first choice and we should grasp it before we forget the meaning of our presence on this earth, which is living life to the fullest.

Recognise that
- Making choices more than anything else is about being clear about what is important to you in life and what you want.
- Making choices is about being capable of voicing your own priorities.
- Making choices is about not being afraid to make mistakes, not being afraid to stick out in the crowd.
- Making choices is about valuing your own voice.
- Making choices is about following your instincts.
- Making good choices for you is about developing sound judgement.
- Making choices is about being assertive.

Self-affirmation
- I recognise that the Creator has willed me the power of choice, and that it is my divine right to exercise my choices as I feel fit, taking care not to infringe on the rights of others.
- I always exercise my right to self-determination and do not allow myself and /or my choices to be determined by any other person.
- I know that my choices may not always be the right ones for me, at the right time; for everybody makes mistakes. However, I reserve the right to make my own mistakes, rather than allow others to make their mistakes at my expense.

* I know that with time, the choices I make will become more seasoned as I gain experience in directing my own life.

Keeping the Dream

I Dream a life in which I am impervious
I Dream a life in which I am my own
definer
I Dream a life in which I can live as my
heart determines
freely following the guidance of my soul.

I Dream a life in which my strength is
renewed everyday

I Dream a life in which my knowledge
grows gainfully

I Dream a life in which obstacles never
throw me off track
but rather I fight back

I Dream a life where I can contribute to my
people's development

I Dream a life in which fear does not
paralyse me, envelope me.

I Dream a life in which I seek my inner
being as the guiding light by which I move

I Dream a life in which all things are
possible, nothing improbable

I Dream a life, which I will make my
reality!

I Dream a life in which I am important
I Dream a life in which I act my own
    desires
I Dream a life in which I am free to grow
    into a person
freely following the guidance of my soul

I Dream a life in which my strength is
    renewed every day?

I Dream a life in which my knowledge
    grows naturally

I Dream a life in which obstacles become
    steps, not blocks
structures I strain against

I Dream a life where I can contribute to my
    healthy development

I Dream a life in which fear does not
    dictate my response

I Dream a life in which ...
    serve as the guiding light by which I move

I Dream a life in which all things are
    possible, nothing impossible

I Dream a life which I will make my
    ...

Keeping the Dream

There is an old Afrikan saying which states *'where there is no vision, the people will perish.'* This is as true of the individual as it is of the collective. The task for you is to maintain your vision of the future and work towards its fruition.

Once you have determined what you want out of life the only way forward for you, Afrikan woman, is up. Identifying the dream is easier if you are in tune with your inner voice, but remaining true to that dream is something else altogether. That takes work and dedication.

Dreams can appear so whimsical that it is easy to discard them as unimportant or unattainable. The most difficult problem that arises in keeping the dream involves remaining in focus and determined. Each one of us must fight not to be swayed by the smaller issues in life, but determine that no matter what our dreams, they can be a reality with a small or large amount of effort on our part. Some people believe that dreams by their very nature cannot become reality. These people believe that dreams are a whimsical fantasy, things that we see when we close our eyes. Sadly, people that have no faith in the power of dreams are the underachievers of this world. They are the progeny of disbelievers, the descendants of those that proclaimed lustily that the pyramids could not be built, that the Nile's food bearing properties could not be harnessed, that Shaka Zulu and his warriors could not defeat the British army, that the Haitians could not defeat Napoleon and that the enslaved could not be free! The Creator gave us the power to dream so that we could realise the true strength of our capabilities in the quiet of the midnight hour.

Dreams are powerful because they can show you the future and they can show the way to solve a difficult problem. Thus one must take the time to understand what dream one wants to follow. Taking time to dream keeps you alive and responsive to life's challenges. It also allows you to reach the heights. It is through our dreams that we are able to comprehend the infinite possibilities in our lives. However, the problem is that many of us become troubled by the challenges this presents to us and seek to escape. Indeed, many of us prefer not to dream at all. We would instead prefer to seek stability and a degree of certainty of what is around the corner. This is fine, if this is truly what you have chosen for yourself. But if, in the quiet hours of the morning, you find yourself yearning for something more, seek it and acquire it. For dreams are there to be made true. Afrikan woman, if you have lost your ability to dream it is time to reclaim it as soon as possible and follow the path that you see defined within your dream.

Sometimes we may be persuaded to give in to things, or to do things that we do not want to participate in. Very often fear of what others think may lead us to do stupid things. Fear of what others might think leads us down the wrong path. So many of us get pulled into the habits of others because we are not always strong enough to maintain our own dreams and aspirations. Unfortunately, there will always be people who will seek to pressurise you to do the things that they do, simply because they feel threatened that you could find life in things that they cannot comprehend. The best thing that you can do for yourself is to remain true to your dreams, and not be drawn into the insecurities of others who wish to make everybody exactly the same as themselves. Many people dislike difference, because it poses dangerous questions to their own belief system, or indicates that there may, just may be, more than one way to tackle an issue. But one of the most profound beauties in life is difference. Seek it, revel in it, and enjoy it. The diversity of life is part of what makes life enduring, forceful and attractive. You are nature's greatest miracle. In this planet of over five billion people, there is nobody exactly like you.

Nature has given you unlimited potential, just waiting to be employed for your own use.

Was there something that you always wanted to do? Perhaps you envisage yourself as an archaeologist, an interior designer, an aeronautical engineer. Whatever dream you see for yourself is attainable. For, if you can conceive of it, you can achieve it.

Recognise that

- Whatever limitations you place on your own capabilities will define you. It is impossible for you to move beyond the limitations that you place upon yourself.
- In disregarding your dreams as inappropriate, or unattainable you may be leaving yourself open to regrets in the future.
- By working dedicatedly towards the fulfilment of your dreams, you will undoubtedly secure for yourself many blessings, be they emotional, financial or spiritual.
- Other people, some of them your family and friends, may choose to do very little with their own opportunities, but you should not allow their lack of vision to limit your dreams.
- Dreams are as valueless as the space they occupy in your mind, if they are not followed by action.

Self-affirmation

- I am the greatest gift of nature. My ability to reason and create makes me so. Thus, my potential is unlimited.
- I do not limit my dreams through fear of other peoples' derision or my own fear of failure.
- I identify my dreams and work dedicatedly towards their fulfilment.
- I commit myself to my dreams and work dedicatedly through action to see them to fruition.

GOALS

The fulfilment of our
    GOALS
    is the ONLY
    scorecard
    by which we may
    chart our
    SUCCESSES

Defining your goals and keeping to them

Goals are the essence of life, the measuring rod by which we may define our successes and failures, and aim to do even better in the future. Therefore, progression in life requires defining your goals and keeping to them. This is the only way to move forward. Defining your goals means knowing what you want and remaining focused upon it. In times of confusion it is no mean feat to keep on target. Life can be so uncertain and without plans it is easy to become like a rudderless ship suspect to the tides of a turbulent sea. Goals are the foundation of any plan. In order to fulfil your life's plan, you will need to have your goals and priorities clearly defined. Life is as uncertain for you as for anybody else. History has shown us the tumultuous times of many Afrikan women's lives, therefore you need to plan as well as anyone else.

If you can imagine for a moment that you intend to take a long journey to a place, a town, another country, where you have never been before. You possess only a limited amount of money for your journey, and a specified time by which you need to reach your destination. How many of us would seriously contemplate commencing this journey without a road map, directions to get to the place of our destination, which signs or routes to follow? We would want to make sure that we arrive at our destination in one piece and in good time. We would not want to arrive late, harassed, broke or in bad health, due to our lack of strategic planning. How much more important are our lives? If we can make the effort to plan our journeys across the country or a world, then why should we not take at least the same care with our lives, which are even more important? We owe that to nobody but ourselves, for very little in this world happens by chance. If you want to at least ensure, with some level of certainty that you will end up where you want to be, then a plan is the only way. The odds are, without one you will wake up too late, in a place where you do not want to be. On the other hand, as the old saying goes, 'if you don't know where you are going, any road will take you there!'

The achievement of your goals will be the singularly most important thing that you will ever do in your life. For through your own hands and efforts you will enjoy the fruits of your own labour. Your emotional state of mind will play a strong role in determining whether you realise your goals or not. Therefore, you must become the mistress of your emotions. Nowadays it seems to be en vogue for people to say or do whatever they like, irrespective of the harm it does to themselves or others, and simply blame it on 'my mood'. Failures are not people who fail every now and again, for we all fail in something at some time, however insignificant or large. A failure is somebody who persistently fails to achieve throughout his or her life. Failures are typically miserable people; they do not control their emotions, which undoubtedly contributed to their failings in the first place. Therefore, if you do not want to consistently fail to achieve your goals you must master your emotions. Whenever you feel a negative emotion, make sure you perform a positive action. Remember to turn each negative into a positive.

I have a close sistah-friend who always manages to do so much with her time. One day I had to ask her, 'How do you do it? How do you juggle the demands of a family life, working part-time, studying full-time, teaching and dedicating time to the upliftment of Afrikan people through organised liberation work?' Her poignant reply was, 'When you want so much for your family, your community and yourself, you will do all that is necessary to ensure that your actions further their development, for that is your ultimate goal.' This means that you organise your life, discipline your time, spend energies on things that matter to you, not on fashion or whimsical notions that have no staying power. Admittedly, studying full-time for a postgraduate degree, working at a demanding bank, teaching at a Saturday school and doing organised community work required significant dedication.

Since a teenager, I have known nothing but plans and goals to reach the heights that I desire for myself. As a teenager I worked hard to save the pennies to buy the things that I wanted that my family could not afford. Now I view work as a welcome ritual in progression, not something to be avoided or disliked. It is simply a process in which you may further yourself and learn, no matter how mundane the task. Today, too many Afrikans view hard work as a curse. It is not in essence, but it can be if you are utilising your skills for people who you don't want to gain from your capabilities, and are being badly paid for it. But each of us has the divine gift from our Creator of making choices, even if we do not see them. Often times when we want to change our lives we want to do it now, this minute. If the changes cannot be immediate we can lose interest in our desire for change, lacking patience to carry through the steps needed to achieve our much needed changes. .

But change seldom works overnight. Most of the time change is not a quick process. Some of us say 'I can't change my job, who is going to pay my rent, my telephone bill, for my car, etc., etc.' Patience is a quality that many of us could learn from our ancestors, who developed it into an art form. We must realise that maybe we cannot change our jobs today, this minute, but we can certainly do so tomorrow or better still create our own job tomorrow. All we have to determine is that this is what we want to do, and it is ours for the taking. We can plan for it, motivate ourselves for this distant goal and achieve it.

Nowadays, when I'm not being productive, I feel dead, dysfunctional, and not in control of my life. Positive action, taken when working towards your goals, acts as an inspiring force for further achievements. Once you have initiated the process of working dedicatedly towards the fulfilment of a goal,

53

and have achieved that goal, you are further motivated towards continuing the process of goal identification and realisation.

Always have a plan, comprising of some goals that you are seeking to achieve. When you have fulfilled each goal move on to your next goal and keep the appointment. You are the pilot of your own destiny. Make sure you know where you are headed in life. Don't leave your destiny to chance. Fasting can be a powerful tool for bringing your goals into fruition. Fast to achieve your plan; throughout the fast concentrate on the positive outcomes that you want for yourself and your loved ones. Fasting is a conscious effort to abstain from taking food, or even liquid in some cases, for a defined period of time. During abstinence from food, the time should be used to concentrate on some aspect of your life which you wish to change or develop. It is important to note, that you should be sure that your body can undergo the stress of reduced food intake, before fasting.

It is important to make a plan for your life, each decade, each year, each month, each week and to maintain it, using it as a guide to define progression or stagnation. These plans should be adaptable to the circumstances of the times. Plans are the food of your life and will help to keep you on track. Always announce your goals to the world. A brotha of mine always says 'word, sound and power,' which essentially means words, when heard, have great power. You need to hear yourself vocalise your desires and goals, for these words act as a motivating force to your spirit and propel you in the direction of their fulfilment. Other people need to hear you say it, to vocalise your goals, for they will be the stick that will beat you if you fail. Therefore, you will work all the harder to avoid the shame that comes with public failure. For those of us with more than our fair share of pride, vocal announcement is a particularly good tool for self-achievement.

Recognise that
- In order to set the right goals for your specific needs you must know yourself intimately. You must know who you

are and what you want out of life. This is different from knowing what your friends, family, colleagues or mate want for you.

- Once you have taken the time and effort to reflect on the challenges of your life and the goals that you intend to set for yourself, these should not be changed without an equal amount of thought and consideration.
- You should always keep a positive mental attitude, and make sure that your environment is conducive to the maintenance of positiveness.

Self -affirmation

- I add to my pool of knowledge everyday, for in doing so I move closer to the fulfilment of my goals. Everyday I ask myself, 'what have I learnt today which was different from yesterday?'
- I do not limit or belittle myself by setting my goals too low. I always set my goals high. I am like a child grasping for the cookie beyond her reach.
- Whenever I feel a negative emotion, I perform a positive action. For example if I feel fear, I push ahead, through the steps, to achieve my goals.
- I always vocalise my goals. Indeed, I shout them from the roof tops for all to hear.
- I form good habits which support the fulfilment of my goals.
- I work hard everyday, as if it were my last opportunity to fulfil my goals. In so doing I move closer to achievement.
- I never procrastinate. If I find myself avoiding tasks, I spring into action immediately, remembering each passing hour is a lost hour from my life, never to be reclaimed.
- Every step I take is a step which brings me closer to the fulfilment of my goals. It is my aim always to add further achievements to my accomplishments to date.

♦ I have a vision for my life, for each decade of my life, for each year of my life. I use my plans as the guiding light for my own development and success.

Determination

Knocked down, kicked back,
Shown up, let down.
Hopes dashed
Hard road
Rainy days
Heavy load
Much blues
doubts cruise.
Fighting hard
Staying true
Keep on track
Never move.
State your case
Move your mind
    Find the opening
        Move inside
Find your locus
Staying focused
    Know your route
        For all else is moot.

Indestructible Me

Some may wonder what pushes me
Why am I focused?
They just can't see
They pursue, they suggest, they try
to decipher me
But still they are remiss
they cannot find the key.
For determined am I
because of my destiny.
Belief in my glorious future,
galvanises me
Thus, definitively determined I will
always be.

The Art of Determination

When things get tough, it's up to you Afrikan woman to keep going and remain focused on your goals, for there are many obstacles that you will have to face in life. The art to it is remembering that what is important is not the number of obstacles you may face, but the way in which you deal with them. Do you run? Do you hide? Or do you face your challenges head on; ready to do what is necessary to triumph? Obstacles are a fact of life and you must not face them with despondency, but with determination, for without challenges there is no life. Therefore, you must understand that life is a challenge, and that challenges are to be triumphed over, or at the very least, tackled. This is achievable through determination and a profound belief in self. Just think how mundane life would be without challenges to spur us on. Admittedly, we are often in turmoil if we are not centred when a challenge arrives, but at the same time we are enriched by the experience. Challenges add to our life experience and in so doing they enrich us. They are simply lessons in living. They enable us to find the best of ourselves, our hidden reserves, which lie unknown to us. Determination is the key to reaching those reserves.

Determination is the tool to self realisation and achievement in life. Through determination, when things get tough you can summon up your bottomless reserves, and continue with what you need to do. Determination is a factor often discounted and taken for granted, but it is something well needed in times of strife, in order to see you through the hard times. Through determination you will persevere and eventually triumph over your obstacles.

Determination is the ability to keep going and push forward when the going gets tough, when you do not achieve what you set out to achieve at your first attempt. Many great scientists, business people, entertainers, professionals, sports personalities, etc., have failed on their first attempt. But their vision, determination and an overwhelming belief in themselves saw them through the difficult times. Most of us will have to be very determined to succeed, and fulfil our hearts desire. Determination is the most important factor for success, for the fulfilment of your goals. For even where the goal seems unattainable, our history is literally littered with examples of those who came before us and persevered through the most difficult circumstances to achieve their goals. They ultimately did this through their determination to not take no for an answer. By not entertaining the often quoted negative 'I can't'. Rather, they shouted, 'I can and I will'. Our ancestors are the most glorious example of that fact. It was through their determination to bath in the sunshine of freedom that led to their triumph over debilitating enslavement of nearly five hundred years. What we must recognise, as individuals on a path to our own fulfilment and personal realisation of our dreams, is that few of us are going to be fortunate enough to have our hearts desires delivered to us on a plate. We will have to work for it and work determinedly and consistently.

Nkechi is a prime example of consistent determination. Nkechi is a woman who has known many hardships in her life, from an early age, when she was orphaned. Nkechi had to fight to gain an education, even though she had limited financial resources to pay her way. But through sheer willpower and resilience, she succeeded in doing so, up to doctoral level. Today, Nkechi is determined to fulfil her ambition of establishing a venture capital bank that will serve the needs of small businesses in Afrika. In so doing Nkechi will give many Afrikan entrepreneurs the chance to fulfil their own dreams. The road to establishing the venture capital bank is not an easy one, and Nkechi has faced many disheartening situations, where her very livelihood has been threatened, as she worked towards her vision single-mindedly. But her determined nature means that there is little doubt that she will succeed in the end.

Determination is the key to achieving all that you have ever wanted to achieve in life. So many of us give up at the first sign of problems. A problem arises in our personal lives or in our working lives and we may feel that great need to run to avoid dealing with difficult issues. Indeed when it comes to problems, our reflexes automatically suggest two possibilities, to fight or to take flight. Given the options we may feel our oncoming problems are so great that the flight response rears its head. But this is not such a great response for finding solutions to a problem. Instead you should view each challenge/problem/obstacle with relish. View it in the light of an opportunity for you to re-assert your worth, your strength, your tenacity, your will power, your ability; all of which Afrikan women hold in abundance.

Nowadays, I do not seek problems, but neither do I shy away from them. To me they represent an opportunity to find out more about myself. It is through our problem solving abilities and our ability to overcome even the greatest trials that we reawaken our natural reserves of tenacity and re-affirm our capabilities. It is an opportunity to grasp.

Recognise that
- Determination is essentially about being resourceful and tapping into your inner strength. It is about pushing yourself beyond whatever you mentally believe is your limit.
- You need to stay focused. Identify where you want to be, check your plan of how you intend to reach your destination, then remain steadfast until you get there.
- Determination is about never saying 'I can't make it'. There is a saying that you need to try a hundred times in order to succeed just once. Few people are lucky (where preparation meets opportunity) enough or brilliant enough to succeed with their first try. Most of us will have to keep knocking at

the door before we make it through. It is determination that gives you the strength to keep coming back to find an opening to what you want to do.

Self-affirmation

- I determine today to do the best that I can in all things.
- I never give up, or stop trying to realise my dreams.
- I have a reserve pool of strength that I can draw on to see me through any difficulties that I may face.
- I know that the best things in life, the things I want the most, seldom come easily. I therefore, keep knocking at the door of achievement, even when I am rejected.
- I know that each rejection that I receive is taking me a step closer to realising my aim. Rejection is merely a rung in my success ladder.

Discipline as Disciple

Discipline is the beating of my drum
in an never ending hum
to ensure that I reach what I want.

Discipline is the nurturing of my mind
to ensure that I find
the strength to continue my fight

Discipline is the get up and go
when others say be slow
to remain on time with my goals.

Discipline is the push to survive
when others take a dive
and triumph over my obstacles in the end.

Discipline is the recognising of my wrong
which prod my spirit like a prong
and cause me to correct my bad moves.

Discipline is the power to make sure
that I do hard things all the more
because I know it is practice for times to
come

Discipline is everything that I need
to ensure that I succeed
in this one life that I live here on earth.

Discipline as Disciple

Discipline is the learning of how to
compel or condition into
a discipline that I teach what I want.

The intimacy the learning of my child
to condition a true
descendant to continue my light

Discipline is the set up and try
out where we no show
to mend or time with my good

Discipline is the push to survive
when others live a diet
to mend over in place leave the emery

Discipline in the mean and dusty
when parents are a burden
and never the second order feed

Discipline is the never a under sure
that in to her I think when more
before a parent is practice the homework
empty

Discipline is everything that I know
for the pure survival
an image the child live over over all

64

Chapter

II

Discipline as Disciple

Its tough remaining disciplined, but we must realise that we are always learning, and the learning stages of life that exist throughout every person's life demand discipline. Discipline is about monitoring yourself, your own performance levels, your own failings and adjusting your behaviour accordingly. It is about wanting the best for yourself and therefore making sure that you complete even the most difficult tasks, to ensure that you succeed in life. Discipline is about doing things not because they are easy, but because they are right for you and will aid you in your development.

These days discipline seems to be a dirty word for many in the Afrikan community. The disciplining of our children is seen as an infringement of our children's rights. A tradition which has never been ours. Discipline is now seen as unimportant, restrictive, un-cool by the young and old. But discipline is a special element in life which teaches us self control and the ability to abstain when and where necessary. Often times it will be a painful experience, but it teaches each one of us necessary lessons. Often times we may enjoy procrastination to avoid disciplining ourselves. Some of us even enjoy putting off the good that will come to us through disciplined action. In order to control this very time consuming habit, one has to be very disciplined. I call it using discipline as your disciple.

It is important that we set the boundaries for our own discipline, and do not leave the task to others. When we look around the world today and observe the many negative situations that people find themselves in, one of the major factors that have led some of them to their negative life experiences has been lack of self-discipline. I am not talking of things which are beyond our control. I am talking about circumstances that we could have avoided. Like drug abuse, alcohol abuse, domestic violence, unruly disrespectful children, low self-esteem. All these factors I believe can be controlled by adults. We have the ability to discipline our children before it is too late. We have the ability, hard as it may seem, to crush domestic violence by saying no and taking disciplined action to ensure that it does not continue. We have the ability to discipline our minds not to accept toxic substances into our bodies. All these factors are within our personal control, we only have to decide to enact self-discipline and affect change.

Afrikan woman you have to pull yourself up when you do wrong, you have to discipline yourself. Nobody is likely to do it as compassionately as you can. We need to retain the habit of disciplining ourselves; self-discipline is the key to any personal achievement. The greatest achievers on the face of this earth have only managed to achieve their aims through self-discipline. Discipline is not as difficult to achieve as we may think it is. So many of us discipline ourselves to wake up each morning, to go to work and collect our salaries at the end of the month. That discipline has been ingrained in us, for fear of not being paid. But just think what bigger riches lay around the corner if we were able to put that same discipline to work for our own development and our own businesses.

Afrikan women have usually been required to be disciplined, for the simple reason that our lives are usually so packed with activity that we need to be very focused in order to ensure that all tasks are completed within the allotted time. So many of us want many things in our lives, but we lack the strength of will to discipline ourselves to create the structures in our own minds which will lead to success. As the saying goes, you cannot reap what you did not sow. And how does the farmer manage to eventually reap her hard labour. By disciplining herself to awake at dawn each morning to start the day's actions of tending to the land; by ensuring that the field is ploughed by a certain time, that the seeds are planted by a certain time and that the harvest is picked by a certain time. Through this disciplined action, a farmer increases the possibilities that her harvest will be bountiful.

Recognise that
- Discipline requires recognising when you are being out of order and correcting yourself accordingly. Discipline is difficult. Indeed it is very painful, especially as a first step, but it is very necessary in order to move up and over. Therefore, you should not always seek the easy option in an attempt to avoid disciplining yourself.
- Discipline can enrich your life in surprising ways. It moves you higher, increases efficiency and increases the respectful light in which you view yourself, which is of the utmost importance for self-esteem and complimentarily increases the respect with which others view you.
- Discipline is a powerful tool not only for you, but for others also. It can inspire others to lift their own discipline levels because of the benefits that they see it brings to you.
- Set yourself goals and tasks and discipline yourself when you do not achieve them. Not harshly, and not just for the sake of it, but with an understanding of what makes you want to improve yourself. Do this with an aim that the self-disciplining measure will have an effect on your future actions, and on you achieving the goal eventually. At the same time it is necessary to be understanding of why you might not have achieved your goal and allow yourself time and space to achieve it.
- Do not punish yourself unduly. Punishment is not the same as discipline. Punishment is a purely subjective reaction to a perceived wrong. Discipline is a subjective understanding of incorrect behaviour/action and a subscribed sanction enacted to rectify the problem.

Self-affirmation

- It is my duty to be my own worst critic. In taking on the task of correcting my own mistakes, it is important that I do not tear myself down. I should always assess my own progress honestly and act accordingly.
- I discipline myself to complete all my tasks in the allotted time.
- I discipline myself to maintain a timetable of action.
- I always remember that self-discipline is divine. It shows that I possess the power to be the mistress of my destiny.

Fear of Success

The spirit within needs release,
I cannot continue to keep it down.

Success, success, success
Success appears to many
as a strange-sounding word.

It sounds like him, not me, never me.
Or even her, the one with the shimmy
and sparkling mind, but no, never me.

For what do I have to offer?
What can I do to bring about this
magnificent feat, success?
How can I capture it?
When shall I find it?
What does it look like?
Hell, why should it be mine?

Success, success, success,
success, it slips off of my tongue,
a melody out of reach.

If only I could make it!
If only I could grasp it,
If only it would be mine!

Perhaps it will, perhaps I can,
maybe its true
that success lies within me
ready to be claimed as my destiny.

Chapter 12

Overcoming the Fear of Success

The Honourable Marcus Mosiah Garvey, leader of the Universal Negro Improvement Association (UNIA) and absolute believer in the genius of Afrikan people, once stated, *"If you have no confidence in self, you are twice defeated in the race of life, with confidence you have won almost before you have started."* Never was a truer statement made about the key to success, the success of the individual and the success of a nation of people.

Unfortunately, many Afrikan women have a fear of success. A fear of the many problems that can arise with being successful in ones professional and/or personal lives. The doubts, the many questions that are posed by those we love, and those we assume love us. The feeling of leaving behind those we would wish to take with us. These are all factors that contribute to the Afrikan woman's fear of success, and act as powerful energy against her personal and professional achievement.

A fear of success in Afrikan women sometimes occurs because we are troubled by the negatives which can and often do arise with the onset of success. Becoming successful means that we are now open to changes in our lives. To most of us change means being vulnerable, an uncomfortable experience for even adventurous people. The feeling of leaving ourselves exposed to the unknown and the unpredictable can be very threatening. So threatening that we might be tempted to lower our standards, or run from success, or even deliberately muck up in order to avoid change. But everything must change;

nothing stays the same, nature and nurture dictates that life must change and progress, as must you, as a part of nature's cycle.

With success, the Afrikan woman becomes vulnerable, is out on a limb, easily separated from the crowd and therefore an easy target. Knowing that it can be a long fall to the bottom, we avoid the possibility of success, for with success can come failure and the long drop to the bottom. Even where we have an idea or a concept that we want to explore, which perhaps nobody else has tried before, we may put off instigating the practice, for fear of not succeeding, or people laughing at us. We may be belittled and devalued to such an extent that we have little belief in our ability to define new boundaries, run our own businesses, start a new profession, or begin to study after a long absence from the educational system.

Many of us may actually believe that success is bad, that you have to be mean, a liar, a cheat or a thief to make it in this world of big money, back room deals and corruption. We may believe that success is dishonourable and you have to fight dirty to make it, or that lack of success or poverty is honourable.

Fear of success in part arises from a lack of self-esteem and lack of belief in self to do the unusual, or to our minds the exceptional. These feelings may be linked to childhood experiences in which we were not given the challenges and support, allowing confidence in our own ability to grow. Childhood experiences are very important in determining the ways in which our self-confidence and self-esteem develops. Afrikan women are not always encouraged by our parents to seek educational achievements which will stand us in good stead, or a business acumen which will allow us to go on and use our own creativity in a business arena. A poor concept of gender roles, known as sexism, has meant that we are often encouraged to do practical things, the secretary not the boss, the nurse not the doctor. Things are changing because some Afrikan women have thrown off these presumed roles and developed their own.

Some of us may want success, but few of us actually believe that it is within our grasp, or capabilities to attain it. In fact many actually believe that we do not deserve to succeed, that struggling is the luck, the kith and kin of Afrikan women. Well there is absolutely nothing noble about living in poverty. There is absolutely nothing wrong with having prosperity and wealth. As Afrikan women we have the right to make positive contributions to the welfare of our families and children through our own positive success.

All of us go through periods in our lives when we believe that we do not have what it takes to be successful. There were times in my life when I would start something unfamiliar or difficult with thoughts of fear of failure ringing in my mind. I would say to myself 'this is too difficult, I've never done this before, what if something goes wrong etc.' But I came to recognise that these statements were limiting my outcomes and I made a concerted effort to stop stating negative things about my abilities. Now when I think of anything that I want to achieve in my life, I visualise myself succeeding, even before I begin the project. I aim to be 100 per cent behind myself. I am not on the sidelines, indecisive, maybe, what if or but. These thoughts lead to failure. I have conditioned myself so much now that I already state that I can, I will and I have never let myself down, because I always try to do the best I can. As time progresses and you come to develop confidence in your own abilities the negative thoughts of failure will rarely visit your door. Each successful task you complete adds to your scorecard, until thoughts of not succeeding become foreign to you. Each success enables you to see further, beyond the horizon.

Recognise that
- If you can conceive of anything, you can create it. Nothing is beyond your grasp.
- Success is already yours; all you need do is claim it. The very fact that you where born is a symbol of the success that is already yours. For, while thousands of your father's

73

sperm never fertilised your mother's egg, one eventually succeeded and allowed you to be brought to life.

- Success is a state of mind; if you do not create the right frame of mind to enjoy your success it will always elude you.
- Fear is a state of mind, not a natural law that you must experience.
- You have a right to success, and a right to good things in life. There is nothing decadent or unworthy about being successful.
- You have a right to good health and well being and not to live a life of struggle and high blood pressure, or diabetes because of a poor diet and harsh physical work.
- You must have confidence in your own capabilities. Develop the confidence to take risks, to stick out from the crowd. Develop good anticipation skills and the agility to move fast when you need to. Develop innovative, yet focused, thinking.
- Success only comes to those who work towards it, to those who persist until they succeed.
- Successful people do the work that failures will not do. They are the people who stay late at the office. They spend extra time researching at their schools so they can learn new skills. They wake up an hour earlier than necessary to concentrate on a new project. They practice their art dedicatedly, all of the time.
- Successful people are never contented with their performance; they always want to do much better.
- Successful people never allow the distance of their journey, or the mountainous terrain to the completion of their goal, to deter them.
- Many Afrikans before you have faced closed doors to opportunity and success, but the faithful learnt how to slide through the cracks.
- Being successful does not necessitate a big fanfare, or blowing of trumpets; for does the sun, the most powerful

energy in the universe, make a sound when she rises each morning?

-
- *Self-affirmation*
- When under stress, facing a new situation, I remind myself of the many times I have triumphed and I turn my mind to concentrating on the task ahead.
- I never contemplate failure or not completing my task. I always visualise myself triumphant and succeeding in my endeavours.
- If I find myself faltering in fear, I act without hesitation, following my instincts and my heart.
- I plan the steps that I need to take to complete my tasks and carry them through diligently.
- I disregard the negative statements or questions posed by the disbelievers in my life, for these are targeted to throw me off track.
- I surround myself with positive people, people who love me and who encourage me and act as positive role models in my life.
- I am an Afrikan woman and I aim for the sky and attain it. My arrow of success is always focused at my star, for if I miss my target and hit the moon instead I am satisfied.
- I act on my ambitions; I do not do myself the injustice of procrastinating, putting off the good that I could enjoy today until tomorrow, for I know that tomorrow may not come.
- I remove all negative language from my vocabulary.
- I understand that any failure that I experience prepares me for the humility of success in the future.
- I know that the upward climb to success merely strengthens my calves for the dancing I will enjoy, when I am at the top of the mountain and enjoying the benefits of an elevated view.
- I never concede to defeat.
- I always persist until I succeed.

Growth

Growth is the lesion that heals
the seed that flowers
the mind that challenges
the organism that decomposes

Growth is life
and when the living die
the well is replenished.

Bitter-sweet-me

I won't deal with people
who hold bitterness to their bosoms
like the last corrupt child
they MUST refuse to discipline.

I hold enough bitterness myself
to satisfy all needs I have
for the sour
to overpower the Sweet.

Growth and Renewal

It always used to puzzle me, that why is it that when you think you have forgiven somebody for some wickedness that you believe they have done to you, that you are then surprised into realising that you still are holding on to the same old bad feelings of unforgiveness and betrayal. You are caught off guard upon being put in a similar situation as that which caused the negative situation, then you realise that those same old feelings still live deeply buried within your emotional make-up. How do you rid yourself of these harmful feelings? These feelings that stop your progress and hold you in limbo, like a puppet being manipulated by old emotions.

To forgive does not mean to forget. It means to recognise that we are all hue-man and make mistakes. We say things or do things that cause bitterness and bad feeling. This is not always because we want to be wicked, but many of us have a tendency to open our mouths before we put our brains into gear. Alternatively we can do quite wicked things for a variety of reasons, such as bad mouth somebody, spreading harmful, malicious gossip which is painful, especially if untrue. These things can be quite destructive to a person's self esteem and trust. Therefore, gossip and bad-mouthing are to be avoided, for they harm not only the person spreading the rumours, by encouraging personal characteristics of slyness, bitterness and dishonesty; but also the person on the receiving end, for they are pushed into a situation of distrust, hurt, betrayal and then faces the ordeal of having to forgive in order to move on. It turns into a classic syndrome of the victim and the victimised, both having to deal with the role they played in helping to create a situation.

However, if you find that you are in a situation where you need to forgive, it is and will always be, the correct thing to do. It is the only way in which to ensure your growth and renewal. You must also remember that if you do not have the capacity to forgive, then how can you expect forgiveness when you do something to upset another person?

Growth and renewal suggest that one needs to exorcise bad feeling. Release it, not breed it until it cripples your emotions. In order to move on you need to release the old and take in the new. You cannot take positive things into your life if your heart is filled with bitterness and hate. Being unforgiving means that bitterness will remain within your heart and stop the good that can come your way. Remember the flooding of your feelings when the person comes to mind, the clouding of the mind as you are faced with the old situations in your memories? These are not feelings that you would want to carry with you for the rest of your life, but they will stay with you unless you forgive.

Forgiveness is an art; it is something that you need to practice often to enable you to forgive at will, when necessary. There are a lot of inhibitions against forgiving. Often times we would prefer to cling to bad feeling. We would prefer to think of ourselves as wronged, hard done by, the victim, the righteous one; and by holding onto these thoughts, we make ourselves out to be a martyr. But martyrdom is for dead people. When you are alive you must act accordingly and use the time that you have on this earth to make your hue-man relationships lasting and full of understanding, rather than reproachful and negative.

More than anything else, forgiveness will mean the ability to move on to a better place and better things, leaving the pain of old problems behind. Reclaiming the new means recognising that old bitterness can only hold you back. Cleansing yourself, by removing feelings of guilt or unforgiveness from your heart means that you have come to an understanding of the wastefulness of an unforgiving spirit, and you want to make room in your heart for love. A good tool used to purge bitterness from the heart is to fast, that is to abstain from consuming food, and to ask yourself for release from your negative feelings.

We all have the capacity to understand the signals that are being sent to us by our friends and assumed foes. We can add to bad signals that are already all around us, due to the aura of unforgiveness and the maintenance of bad feelings; or alternatively we may throw good signals back out, even when this may not be our intuitive response. You'll be surprised at what comes back at you. If we give to others lightness, laughter and friendship, they will return more of the same in abundance. Have you ever heard the saying 'like attracts like' It is true, birds of a feather do flock together.

So many people would love to be in the luxurious position of having the capacity to forgive on demand, but do not know how to do so. So long have they been holding on to their feelings of bitterness and resentment that, in some cases, it becomes such a habit that the breaking of this cycle becomes a difficult task to accomplish. The best way to deal with this difficulty is to take each day at a time and nurture yourself out of the habit, through projecting pleasant images of your most unforgivable situation or perceived foe. This will get you used to seeing the person in a positive image, rather than antagonistically. Eventually, you will find yourself being able to accept the person as one deserving of forgiveness.

Recognise that
- I find it so difficult to forgive because I want to remain in the right, while my presumed adversary is wrong.
- I lament and reflect on the experience which led to the unforgiving situation, to such an extent, that it is with me at all times.
- I feel righteous when I hold onto my feelings of resentment, and for a while it makes me feel good. I really dislike the person that I need to forgive. I enjoy disliking that person. I

get a rush of adrenaline when I reminisce, which I do not want to let go of.

- My anger gets in the way of dealing with the issue which led to the bad relationship between me and my perceived adversary.
- I believe I don't know how to forgive even if I wanted to, so it is easier for me to continue the way I am with my feelings of resentment, rather than challenge myself to improve.
- I often solicit support from others around me in order to justify holding onto feelings of bitterness.
- I feel depressed and dejected when I think about the situation and wish that it had never occurred. But I do not know what to do for the best, to remove my feelings and resolve the situation.
- Because I feel bitterness towards another person, I need to purge my heart and ask for release from my negative feelings. Fasting, the abstinence from food, is a good process for releasing negativity.
- I recognise today that many times in my life I have harmed somebody, sometimes unintentionally, by thoughts or actions and have thus required forgiveness. Thus in return I must do the same for somebody else.

Self-affirmation

- I practise forgiving somebody everyday. I forgive myself for any indiscretions I may have committed against somebody else. I forgive all those I remember having wronged me. I do this even when I feel that it is having no effect. But still I maintain thoughts of love for myself and the people I need to forgive.
- I know that forgiveness is the only true way to come to terms with hurtful situations and release myself from bitterness, to move on and to grow.

- I have decided today, that I no longer wish to be an unforgiving person. I make a promise to myself that I intend to do everything in my power to forgive all those that I believe have harmed me, intentionally or unintentionally.

The Greenest Eye

Green is the colour of my pain when
I covet that which I cannot gain.
I look to others instead of myself
for true happiness and understanding

Green is the colour of my pain when
I desire what others have
I find fault in my own properties
and possessions
which only leads to animosity
or even aggression

Green is the colour of my pain when
I fail to look for the
root of my dissatisfaction
instead I transpose my feelings
I give others the blame
to avoid my shame.

Yet I,
Afrikan woman
have the power to change,
to feel all colours of the rainbow,
and I will .I will.

Mastering the Greenest Eye

Every person on this earth has the capacity to experience jealousy. Not one of us is free from this destructive emotion. It can hit us at the most unexpected of times, in the most unexpected places, over the most trivial of issues. Jealousy is normally experienced within the gender group rather than across gender, for we generally compare ourselves with those we desire to be like. Through the barrage of assaults Afrikan people have experienced from racist onslaught there is also a tendency to compare oneself wittingly across racial lines. Therefore, more and more Afrikan women may find themselves comparing their beauty to the perceived beauty of the European female, the straightness of the nose, the thinness of the lips, the texture of the hair etc. Such a comparison is pointless, because one is not comparing like to like, and can also be harmful and emotionally destructive in these perilous times of bigotry.

Few of us have developed the technique to overcome these feelings of jealousy. Invariably you will find that within those of us who have developed the capacity to defeat jealousy, there's a profound belief in the Creator, and an understanding beyond the material, beyond the here and now. Often times this capacity will be tied to a spiritual belief system, a clear relationship with the Creator, and an understanding of our space in time.

Like most people, for the Afrikan woman, jealousy is a mechanism used to express all the disappointments and dissatisfactions we view within our own lives and give them outlet. Instead of dealing with the source of our disappointments, we have a tendency to give them life by masquerading them as an alternative emotion, i.e., jealousy, and then project them onto somebody else who we feel is living a life 'better, more comfortable, more beautiful, more intelligent, etc., than our own.' These feelings of jealousy may be tied to anything, anytime, anywhere.

Jealousy may rear its head when one finds oneself in situations similar to childhood occurrences in which jealousy was a dominant emotion expressed. This might be feelings of inadequacy, awkwardness, ugliness, stupidity, fatness, etc. Where this is the case, in which negative childhood situations are replayed, the Afrikan woman finds herself vulnerable. It then becomes a simple step to allude to a person she feels does not encompass the negative persona that she perceives herself to hold.

Jealousy may be tied to status within society, it may be tied to perceived beauty, it may be tied to definitions of intelligent behaviour, athletic ability, artistic talent, professionalism, popularity, etc. There are so many factors that can lead to the expression of jealousy, which can dominate lives and makes relationships with our sistahs difficult. Afrikan women tend to be more susceptible than others to the phenomenon because, more than any other, we are the ones who are socio-economically located at the bottom of the ladder, and therefore with the greatest number of obstacles and forces fighting to keep us down. We are therefore faced with more people to define as the 'haves', and ourselves as the 'have-nots'. However, jealousy does not solve our problems and logically, with so many random factors which can lead to jealousy, and the lack of ability to remove these factors which are a fact of life, the only solution is to destroy the feelings of jealousy that live within all of us.

We would be better served by recognising the limitations that we perceive within our own lives, and bridging those gaps by filling them with the substance that we always wanted. Certainly by this I am not giving reference to the wild rush to acquire material goods and wealth, but the spiritual fulfilment that we find missing within our own lives.

Most Afrikan women find it difficult to admit to themselves, let alone to anyone else, that they are feeling jealousy. But one of the better ways to deal with the emotion is to firstly identify that you are feeling it, and then move on to how you are going to remove it. But if you deny that it even exists, then it will not be possible to identify a course of action to eradicate it and its attendant negative vibrations. Jealously to that extent is very similar to alcohol abuse. You first have to admit that you are abusing before you can deal with the abuse effectively.

So many friendships between Afrikan women are destroyed because of quite petty jealousies which, had they been controlled and identified as such, would have not inhibited those relationships from developing further.

There are so many stories that can be told in this regard, one of which is the story of Amina and her close friend Npeti. Amina met Npeti when Npeti joined her law mooting (debating) society at her London University in which they were both studying law. Amina had been attending the law mooting sessions for a year since the beginning of her course, and had built up quite a following within the society due to her quite sound mooting skills. Npeti had just transferred from another London university and was new to the society. Both women took an immediate liking to each other and began to form a sound friendship. However, six months into the relationship things started to go wrong when Npeti, having settled into her new environment, began to shine at the law mooting sessions. She proved to be quite a remarkable debater, with a naturalness rarely seen on the debating platform. Members of the society, of which there were some two hundred people, began to show her attention and congratulate her. This was attention which had previously been showered on Amina, who now felt denied her 'role'. She felt she had been usurped by the newcomer and began to distance herself from her new friend, because she did not know how to masquerade and deal with her painful emotions. At first Npeti was not aware of her friend's emotions, but over the course of three months as Amina became more and more evasive and their conversations became shorter and filled with tension, Npeti understood that something was wrong. Amina, on the other hand, having dishonestly denied her feelings of jealousy, became deeply entranced by them. She was unable to surmount them or even discuss them with Npeti because she could not even identify them to herself. She became bitter. Her speech to Npeti became sharper and malicious when addressing her as well as when addressing other people about Npeti. Amina eventually began to ignore Npeti when they were both in the company of others, behaving in an animated manner, perhaps in an attempt to make Npeti jealous of her vivaciousness.

Npeti, still unclear as to why her friend was behaving in such a hurtful manner, began to withdraw from Amina and maintain her distance. In the meantime Amina's jealousy had exploded; she now began to perceive other things about Npeti which were worthy of her jealous feelings. Thus, although a very beautiful woman, Amina began to notice and be jealous of Npeti's beauty. She began to notice the way Npeti walked, the other friends Npeti had, the way Npeti made people laugh, the positive things people had to say about Npeti. Thus the classical jealousy syndrome had overtaken Amina; she had began to explore her jealousy unconsciously, and notice justifications for her jealousy by looking at other characteristics of the object of her jealousy.

Over a period of a further six months Amina had totally destroyed her promising lifetime friendship with Npeti, due to her uncontrolled feelings of jealousy. Her feelings of intense jealousy still remain with her today even though she and Npeti severed all ties many years earlier. Distressingly, every time she meets or sees somebody who reminds her of Npeti, the same feelings of jealousy raise their bitter head and belittle her self-esteem.

There are two main concepts that define the process of jealousy. These are projection and reaction formation.

Projection means I turn my feelings of dislike for somebody into their dislike of me, so that I may justify my emotions. This leads me to blame my assumed foe for perceived wrongs that they have done to me. Reaction Formation means that although I desire something, I convince myself that I do not, in order to guard my emotions from the knowledge that I cannot attain the thing that I desire.

Recognise that

- Jealousy is a terrible emotion that I feel. It grips my entire person and leads me to irrational thoughts and behaviour.
- It leads me to evaluate my life in comparison to the person I am jealous of. Oftentimes my feelings of intense jealousy are more linked to my complex personality, than they are to the person who is the object of my jealousy.
- My jealousy is based on an assumption about the life of the person I am jealous of. This perception of another person's life may be well founded, but it is usually inappropriately compared to my own, and therefore bears no resemblance to reality.
- My jealousy is a debilitating emotion which needs to be checked and brought under control by me.
- I find myself feeling vulnerable when I come into contact with somebody who has attained something that I always wanted, be it education, material goods or a man. I then find myself making unjustified comparisons between myself and my now defined 'adversary', the one who has what I want. I will find myself wanting in this comparison, which makes me feel even more vulnerable, which in turn rears feelings of jealousy within me and a desire "to be like" or "have some of what she has".
- Often times my jealousy is aroused when I covet that which does not belong to me. I covet that which is attractive to me, be it a hue-man being or an object. I covet that which is beyond my access because I know that it is unobtainable to me and therefore I want it all the more.

- I am friendly in public to those I feel most jealous of in a subliminal fashion, in order to disguise my feelings of jealousy from myself and others. But deep down I am not comfortable in their presence.
- I try to belittle and undermine the person I feel jealous of at every opportunity, and I encourage others to do the same.
- I often project my feelings of jealousy onto those I feel jealous of. I convince myself, in a reaction to hide my feelings of inadequacy from myself, that the person in question really dislikes me and is acting badly towards me, not vice versa.
- I try to make others dislike those I feel jealous of in my need to solicit support.
- I can be very bitter and mean towards those I feel jealous of, although they have caused me no harm.

Self-affirmation
- To overcome this problem I must first be honest with myself and admit that I have the capacity to suffer from jealousy.
- I recognise that the things I sometimes want are not necessarily good for me.
- I do not measure my own achievements against other people. I am unique and therefore my attributes are unique.
- I understand that I am my own best rival.
- I note my own characteristic first signs of jealousy so that I can use them as an early warning signal of my impending discomfiture.
- I do not harm others through my inconsiderate and hurtful actions, expressed because of my jealousy.
- I practise every day, telling myself of my many special attributes, my uniqueness.
- I understand that anything I want can be mine. I do not need to be envious of anybody in order to fulfil my own needs.
- I am mistress of my emotions.

Quiet Time

Listening to your inner spirit
can be frightening
challenging
and infinitely quiet.
YET
it is the only route
to true knowledge of self.

Let Spirit be Your Only Guide

You must listen to the voice from within, as a guide to a stronger, healthier life. Spirit is a function of the inner soul which works in unison with mind, to keep us in touch with the cosmos.

By quietly listening to the voice within we can determine what is good for us, even under times of stress and uncertainty. Many people are afraid of silence and in fact will do anything to avoid it. Such as switch on the TV, switch on the radio, talk on the telephone, anything but listen to our own voices. When I was a child I loved to listen to my silence, to converse with myself, to ask myself questions and listen patiently for the answer. As I grew I lost that ability in the bustle of life. By the time I reached university I was jumping off the walls, just like everybody else. Until the end of my second year at university, when living in an isolated area on my own, I was forced to listen to the voice within for the simple reason that there was nobody within easy reach to distract me. It was during this time that I eventually came to an understanding of what I wanted out of life, and what actions I could take to make sure that my dreams were realised. I only came to that understanding through listening to my inner voice; spirit spoke to me and showed me the way, giving me the desire to seek that which is mine.

Listening to the inner voice of spirit is no mean feat. There are many learned responses that we take from society, which condition us to discard spirit and deal only with the scientifically defined. This is the wrong system to work by. Spirit is the only force which can keep us in tune with our

Creator. If we follow spirit, we are following the guidance of the creator. Without spirit it is easy, in fact, more than likely to lead to deadened choices and unhealthy positions in life. Only spirit can guide the Afrikan woman to her rightful place in this life.

I believe in the force of the Creator one hundred per cent. I believe that the force which created all life is beneficent and altruistic. I believe that this force, spirit lives within all living things, from the trees that whistle in the wind, the birds, and the mammals including hue-man kind, the marine life, and the ocean. All life is due to the force of the Creator, known as Oludumare, Mwari, Amon in Afrikan belief systems. As hue-mans we have the greatest capacity to live our lives in the image of our Creator. We have the greatest capacity to visualise and enact the best that we can be. Many of us are not harnessing that God-given capacity. It is not necessary to be a religious person, by which I mean follow any of the established leading religious doctrines, in order to believe in the Creator. In fact, it is true that these doctrines have been used the world over to destroy people and justify genocide and ungodly practices. Christianity was used by the European to enslave Afrikans for nearly five hundred years, to steal our lands and to colonise Afrika under the guise that we were/are 'heathen'. Christianity was used by the European to commit acts of genocide against the people of the New Afrikan Islands (known as the Caribbean or West Indies, both of which are misnomers). Christianity was used by the European to commit genocide against the people of the Americas, who now mainly live in concentration camps (euphemistically known as reservations) in America, a tragedy which has been brushed under the carpet. Indeed, Christianity has been used by the European even against himself, for no other reason other than the desire to rule the world through christian dictatorship. The armies of Constantine quite successfully enforced this during the 6th century C.E.

Islam has been and continues to be used by the Arab to enslave Afrikan people and steal our lands. It was used by the

Arabs during the 'holy wars' known as Jihad, particularly as perpetuated across North and West Afrika 1500 C.E. Today, Islam is being used to justify the enslavement of Afrikans and the stealing of Afrikan lands in the Sudan, in Chad, and distressingly in Mauritania, where slavery for some Afrikans is a way of life and is justified under Islamic law. Let me stress this once more, Afrikans are still living in slavery in Mauritania and in the Sudan. They are wholly owned by their masters and have no rights to self-determination. These Afrikan people are enslaved today, just as our ancestors were enslaved as chattel, centuries ago. Islam has been a barbaric experience for Afrika. Today one-third of Afrika, is Islamic, and this was achieved through bloodshed and brutal conversion on threat of death. Today in the Sudan, many Afrikans who are defined as animist are refusing to convert to Islam and the Sudan military regime, run by Arabs, has been bombarding these people with prolonged acts of genocide. The situation in the Sudan is not one of Christian Afrikan fighting, Islamic Afrika, as the Arabs would love to depict it. Rather, there are traditional Afrikan spiritualists fighting alongside Afrikan Christians, and some Afrikan Muslims, against the Arabs who largely populate the northern part of the country. The Arabs seem particularly keen to kill or enslave the Nuba people who originally populated many northern areas of the country, but have been forced to migrate southwards in an vain attempt to avoid the barbarity of the Arabs. However, unfortunately many of them have been enslaved and the Nuba continue to lose part of their heritage every day as they have been removed from their traditional cultural and ancestral grounds.

Afrikan people do not need to belong to any religious order to believe in the Creator. Religions are dictated by man. You need to be dictated to by your inner spirit. The two are not the same. One need not be afraid to seek spirit over religion. Be secure in the knowledge that your inner spirit will guide you, regardless of whether you attend church every Sunday or go to mosque every Friday. Be secure in the knowledge that yes, the Bible and the Koran contain some truths that one has to find behind the interpretations of its messengers; but the original book of spiritual belief, the book of "Coming Forth by Day," misnomered the 'book of the dead', contains far more unadulterated truths and rules by which we might guide our lives to a spirited existence. The book "Coming Forth by Day" is the original book of life and comes from the ancient Kemetian (Egyptian) system of spirituality and self governance. It precedes the existence of the Bible and the Koran.

Spirit means remaining quiet and focusing on the substance that comes from within, not the noise that comes from without. Often times that noise is contributed to by the noise of religion. Take the time to understand what goodies destiny has in store for you if only you would follow the right course. People sometimes ask, 'When do you know that the message you receive after meditation is the right one for you?' The answer is simple. Meditation causes you to focus on your inner strength and wealth of knowledge that is hidden in the depths of your mind. When you call on that force, it will always give you what you require. The answer will come to you quietly and without conflict or 'but', or 'what ifs'. Then you will know that it is the right answer for you. Listening to your inner voice can be a traumatic experience, just because it is new to many of us. Problems, habits and insecurities will rear their head, trying to throw you off track. But the most revolutionary thing we can do at this time is to recognise our resistance to change and fight to overcome that resistance.

Recognise that
- You must stop living your life guided by individuals who do not know what is best for you. If you listen to your inner spirit you will determine what is best for you, as only you can.
- The Creator loves you and will never forsake you in times of need, difficulty or pain.
- When you feel distracted or unfocused, concentrate on meditating to remove the feelings, and to find your centre once again. Even if you do not feel to do so, force yourself

98

anyway, you will be surprised at the results. Never allow feelings of lack of focus to stay with you as they have the ability to throw you off track indefinitely.

- When in serious doubt, or serious difficulties, use the force of libation to call on the name of your great ancestors (they do not have to be your ancestor by lineage, as long as they are of your same cultural background) to assist you in your search for peace and clarity, and to help you resolve your problems. Your ancestors will always guide you but they can only assist you if you call upon them with water (fire and alcohol, food etc., may also be used). Pouring libation is an ancient Afrikan tradition which still exists today, as an intrinsic part of the Afrikan psyche. It is a remembrance that 'you are, therefore I am' and a thanksgiving to that fact.

- The quest for your inner spirit can be best achieved by utilising the simple term 'be still and know.'

Self-affirmation

- I do not listen to the clamour of voices from without, but rather, focus on those from within.
- I am not put off by the fact that I might be alone in seeking this course for myself. To be alone does not mean to be wrong.
- I understand that I was born of the spirit and therefore I must live from the spirit.
- I use my spirit as my guiding light, as my source of direction and I follow its messages diligently.
- I take some quiet time each day, just to listen to the calling of my spirit.
- In times of conflict I meditate for direction.
- I am Creations greatest miracle and I give thanks to that fact everyday.

for all my sistahs who hate their hair when the crown is enuff

Crackling like fire
electricity runs through
Fusion like science
everyday feel brand new
warm and curly
smelling so sweet
moistly textured
whether elongated or petite
Keep mine shining
brightly in the sun
never afraid to define
myself and simply have fun.

ROOTS

I am AFRIKAN woman
I wear my natural hair with PRIDE
I know the value of my CROWN
For I am QUEEN
The FIRST
The LAST

My beautiful hair is God-given
For all to see and admire
It is the height of my evolution
a statement of my passion
My glorious Afrikan hair
traces my divinity in this life
It is the map of my past
The course of my future

It is the here and now,
I am Alpha and Omega.

My clean scalp is the route of the Nile
which electrified the world
My roots are the beginnings of the mind
that created Civilisation
My tightly sprung curls are the music
which set the pace of the crafting of all monuments exclaiming
the glory of my Ancestors.

I recognise the divinity of all of me
I care for my tresses; I don't destroy or stress it
No chemicals or lye for me in a vain attempt to look de-natured
and un-hueman

NO!
I refuse to harm the beauty that is me.
Instead, I comb, twist, tease, pluck, groom, squeeze
I grease and nurture my illustrious, divine Afrikan hair
For I KNOW its value
and I CARE!

Chapter
16

Natural Woman: The Crowning Glory of Afrikan Hair

"You make me feel, you make me feel, you make me feel like a natural woman." The singing of this revolutionary song sums up the feeling of natural beauty and its many blessings, health-wise and spirit-wise. Keeping your hair natural allows you to be in touch with who you are as an Afrikan person, it keeps you in touch with the inner you. Not all of us see the ready benefits of being natural and in touch with our lives and indeed, many would proclaim that destroying the natural contours of Afrikan hair does not condition the mindset of the person, but I believe otherwise. I maintain my natural hair for the betterment of my health and as a conscious effort to counter the annihilation of Afrikan beauty and cultural forms.

Some dreadful things have happened to us as Afrikan people over the past 500 years. The onslaught has been fierce, so very fierce in the last one hundred years that we now perceive perming and other chemically de-constructive techniques to be the norm for Afrikan hair. Many of us even fail to question why we want to perm our hair, we just do it. And even more harmful nowadays, we also do it to our children without thinking through the harm that it is doing to the growing child. The perming of Afrikan hair is now perceived as a 'rites of passage' for Afrikan teenage girls and even boys. It is acceptable as the done thing to perm our young teenagers' hair when they reach a certain age, to show that they are moving into adulthood. Even more disturbingly it is now conceived by many mothers as an 'easy' way out of the maintenance of her child's natural hair. It is true that some children experience stress when having their natural hair combed, perhaps because their hair is beautifully thick and luscious. These children, in experiencing pain in their scalp, transmit their suffering to their parents and of course, no responsive parent likes to see their child suffer. So a solution is sought, as it should be. Finding the solution requires that the parent first of all identifies what the problem is. Due to our inexperience, and more importantly the poor hair care products on the market, it is easy for us to jump to the erroneous conclusion, that it is our child's hair that is the problem. But in actual fact, the quality of moisturiser used in the hair, which might more appropriately be called grease, the technique used when combing the hair, and/or the quality of the comb that is used, is more likely to be the problem.

The harmful process of perming our hair has never been presented to us as a reasoned case of why to perm, providing detailed information of what it does to Afrikan hair and skin. Instead, company advertising sells to us the many 'benefits' of perming, namely looking like that, other than what we are. We seem to pick up cues from our parents and peer group that this is the done thing to do when we reach a certain age. Few of us have the foresight to extend critical analysis and ask 'why?' I know I did not.

I remember the first traumatic experience of first destroying my natural hair. I did it for the simple reason that I did not know what to do with my hair. I was fourteen years old and my mother, due to her demanding work commitments as a single parent, had stopped involving herself in the maintenance of my hair, declaring that I was old enough to care for it myself. However, I had never had any experience of maintaining my hair. If the truth be told I could barely plait my own hair. For a year I struggled to maintain my hair, often going to school with scruffy unkempt plaits that failed to last the course of the day. I was not picked on for doing so by my peers, but of course I noticed the difference between my hair and the seemingly smooth, shining straight texture of my friends' hair, some of whom had been perming from the age of ten years. Of course I was as susceptible to advertising as anybody else at the age of fifteen. I certainly did not know of the damage of perming, a fact which for obvious reasons is kept very quiet, lest profit margins are affected. At the age of fifteen I got fed up of struggling to maintain my hair, a task which, to my shame I had never taken the time to learn and so I decided to perm. It was the worst decision I had ever taken in my young life. My fine delicate hair could not handle the strength of the perming agents which stung and burnt until I thought I would scream. My hair broke for a full month after that experience until it finally stopped breaking. I did not really care to keep perming after that but there never appeared to be a good alternative, so I continued perming my hair, but I was never happy. I continued perming off and on, alternating with long extension plaits, until the age of 22 years when I gave it up forever. The best move that I ever made. As I became politically aware I was able to articulate the unease that I had always had with perming my hair, the intense feeling that it just was not me. I did not feel like who I am when I was perming. I never felt so free and alive as the day that I made up my mind never to perm again.

When I had the experience of touching my natural hair for the first time in almost seven years I nearly cried with the joy of the experience. I felt so alive; the experience was sensual and exciting. There is no feeling on earth like the feeling that you get through your body when you brush your natural hair. For me, it is like a soft tingling sensation, running down your spine, similar to that feeling that I get when I am attracted to a fine Afrikan man.

Most Afrikan women and men who perm their hair do not consciously do it in a desire to appear European; which would be following in the tradition of why the perm was created by an Afrikan-American woman in the first place. We do it because for as long as our memories can remember, most Afrikan women have always done so, or at least the so-called 'glamorous' or 'beautiful' ones have. We forget the reason behind why the first Afrikan women chose to perm their natural hair; and in following those first Afrikan women without questioning why, we blindly fall into the trap of perming for the same reasons as those original women, to look other than the way the Creator originally created us. We need to question why do we perm our hair? Is it for traditional reasons? What tradition? How long has this tradition been in existence? Where did it come from, this tradition? Why did the tradition come into being? These are the questions that any intelligent person asks in trying to understand why they are participating in something. These are questions that every Afrikan woman and man perming her or his hair needs to ask themselves, and listen carefully for the answer. Is it enough to follow a tradition blindly? Or is it time to stop and develop a more healthy tradition, which is based on a respect of the way in which the Creator made all Afrikan people, with kinky, beautiful, curly hair.

The destruction of Afrikan hair works on a sub-conscious level. We make excuses that destroyed hair is easier to maintain, that our hair is not manageable, that it is stronger, more versatile, it grows quicker with perming. All of these statements are simply bogus. In reality it has been established that natural hair is four times stronger than chemically altered hair; and grows at an average rate of half an inch each month, a growth rate which has not be accelerated by the use of chemicals.

Everything in nature is created with the ability to reproduce itself, in its original created image. Yet we Afrikans would believe that the Supreme Creator gave us life with a crop of hair that we could not manage and which needs to be chemically treated, while the Asian and Caucasian required no such treatment. Are we, therefore, suggesting that the Supreme Creator in creating the original, the first woman and man on earth, who were undisputedly the Afrikan woman and man, made a mistake with our hair? The Supreme Creator did not make a mistake with the creation of the great oceans, the forests and the stars, but when it comes to Afrikan hair we would believe that something went dreadfully wrong.

The maintenance of Afrikan hair in its natural state is the easiest thing imaginable. We need only wash, moisturise and brush and style natural hair. Whereas with permed hair, the texture and natural contours of the hair have been so destroyed and changed that one needs to do all manner of things to make sure that the hair does not drop out. This involves expensive steams with additional chemicals to maintain the permed look, the use of harsh curlers to straighten the hair, but at the same time trying to give it body, the use of chemical based moisturisers to try to keep the dried out hair moist, an almost impossible task for deconstructed hair. Curly perms are even more destructive because of the action of heat with the chemicals on hair. The main ingredient in curly perms is thioglycollic acid, which can cause burns and severe skin damage.

Damage limitation due to the hair problems that occur through perming costs an incredible amount of money on a yearly basis. When the natural re-growth appears, the hair becomes even more unmanageable, as it is difficult to comb, for combing entails trying to reach the roots of the hair that are thick, but at the same time the force of combing through the natural hair, then means that as the comb comes into contact with the permed hair, the force is too harsh and the permed hair can tend to break. Therefore, one finds many sistahs running to hairdressers for a retouch. The space of time between these retouches seems to get shorter and shorter, meaning that sistahs are allowing more volume of chemical onto their hair on a yearly basis leading to long term scalp and hair problems as time passes.

Contrary to popular belief, permed hair does not grow faster than natural hair. In fact chemicals can irritate the scalp and roots of the hair to the extent that the growth process of Afrikan hair slows down. Afrikan hair grows at its own rate of half an inch each month, until it reaches its threshold, which is different for different people. No amount of chemicals will increase the speed at which our hair grows. On the contrary, it can slow it down, for it can clog our pores, which leads to less oxygen reaching the roots of our hair. Lastly, Afrikan hair is the most versatile of all hair. Its thick texture and strength means that a variety of styles may be achieved, including plaiting, twisting, dredding, carving, and dying. The versatility of Afrikan hair is easily demonstrable by the simple fact that through the use of chemicals we can get our hair to appear Caucasian-like, but no amount of chemicals would allow a Caucasian or an Asian to achieve an Afro. If that sad fact does not prove the versatility of Afrikan hair, I don't know what will.

Afrikan hair is strongest when left in its natural state. The deconstruction of Afrikan hair through chemicals can aggravate all kinds of problems like eczema, psoriasis, contact dermatitis and total baldness, i.e., folliculitis, in which hair cannot grow through scarred tissue as the follicules are closed by hardened skin. Permanent scalp damage, burning of the scalp and skin, as well as scarring are further side effects. Skin problems often occur due to the chemicals coming into contact with facial and neck skin. In fact some people develop eczematous skin conditions with frequent exposure. Even cancer has been said to be linked to the toxic chemicals used in the production of these perming chemicals. Are all these problems really worth looking Caucasian?

Unfortunately, the Black hair 'industry,' having made a lot of money out of the desire for Afrikan men and women to alter their natural state, are now moving on to even greater profits by targeting our children with so-called 'kiddies kits.' It is sad to say that many mothers and fathers are falling into the trap or allowing their children as young as one year to have their hair permed! What madness, soon we will be looking for ways to perm our babies' hair while they are still in the womb. The Afrikan child's hair is so delicate that it should not be permed, it is porous and soft. Thus, the use of chemicals at these young ages can be so detrimental that the child's hair may never recover. Our children have now become pawns in an industry seeking to make profits over and above the welfare of any Afrikan child. Be on your guard that these 'kiddies packs' used to perm children's hair contain sodium hydroxide (lye), also known as caustic soda. It contains as much as 1.2% with a pH of 14.3, which is toxic to a child of four. This sodium hydroxide is an alkali, which is typically used in the chemical industry for acid neutralisation. It is used in the refining of oil, removing hair from blocked drains and even as a cleaning agent. Inhalation can lead to respiratory problems and damage of lung tissue. Ammonium hydroxide is also present within relaxers/perms and this can typically be found in household cleaners - cleaners incidentally, for which you are advised to wear gloves!

Mothers, ask yourselves this question, 'why does the Black hair 'industry' advise Afrikan women not to perm when pregnant, nor up to three months after pregnancy?' Is it for the simple risk of harming the child being carried and the damage that you may do to your own hair when perming soon after carrying a child, which alters the structure of your body. Surely if perming was absolutely safe one would be able to perm regardless of whether one was pregnant or not.

Afrikan woman you need to care for your hair, not destroy it. When you nurture your hair you will feel on top of this world.

Recognise that

- Your hair is a core part of who you are and therefore requires maximum care and protection.
- Your hair keeps you in tune with the cosmos. Your hair contains melanin, the pigment which reacts with the sun and sound waves. Therefore, your natural hair better enables you to communicate with nature.
- Permed hair, chemically treated, is dangerous because the chemicals within the hair react with the sun.
- Children deserve a childhood, not to be made up in the image of adults. Avoid perming children's hair.
- You will have a better chance of succeeding in changing from permed or chemically treated to natural hair if you identify a natural hair mentor to assist you. They will assist you with the changes your body will go through and the

mental conflicts. A natural hair mentor is somebody who understands natural hair processes, or somebody who has positively made the transition from permed/chemically treated hair to natural hair.

Self-affirmation

- I aim to find out the true impact of chemically treated hair on my body, if I am perming.
- I love and care for my hair, just as I love and care for my body in general.
- I promise to give myself time to nurture back my natural hair, once I decide that this is what I want. I am not impatient as I move towards natural hair, but rather understand the changes that my mind and body are going through in taking this important step.
- I do not bow to societal and/or peer pressure, which may urge me to keep perming or chemically treating my hair, if I decide this is not what I want to do.
- I allow the children in my life the opportunity to make their choices about chemically treating their hair, only when they are young adults, and after I have provided them with all the facts, so that they may make informed decisions.

Living in the Light

i pledge myself to my Maker
in all things at all times.
i recognise through you that i have life.
Supreme Creator, through your
everlasting presence i live
and therefore i must give.
Give me the strength to love you
as the giver of life and to
honour my ancestors, my mother
and father as the seed that
gave me existence.
i look within myself to find the light,
which I need to fully exist.
i pray that i always seek to remain
bathed in the glorious sun
that is the symbol of
your everlasting presence.

Spiritual Renewal and Upliftment

Dedicating yourself to spirit and using your person as an instrument of creativity can only lead you to renewed blessings and upliftment, to surpass your wildest dreams. Living from the spirit requires reaffirming your commitment to inner peace and rejuvenation. In so doing you will come to understand your purpose on this earth. If you are at a point where you do not know what your purpose is, living from the spirit will enable you to find one.

A key to living from the spirit is giving. Giving to those less fortunate than you is the greatest gift that one can give in life, other than giving life itself. We may feel that we do not have much to offer, but we can surprise even ourselves. We can give of our creativity, of our time, of our energy, of our inspiration. It may not necessarily be giving our money or possessions. We can give whatever we have at the most unexpected of times and many blessings will be returned our way.

I give what I can, because of the joy of giving, the feeling of enlivening somebody else's life through my generosity. There is a Yoruba proverb that says the grandmother asks for a piece of yam from her grandchild, not because she wants the food, but because she wants to determine the spirit of the child, whether the child will be mean or giving, and to teach that child the joy of sharing, an important lesson for all of us. Many of us are still learning that lesson. Some of us will never realise it. Some of us may equate giving unconditionally with being taken advantage of, being taken for a ride, being used and abused, because we do not recognise that it is not the giving itself which is important, but the spirit in which you give. A sister who epitomises this giving nature is Lamlam, a woman who never hesitates to give what she can to those who touch her heart. Whether Lamlam gives financial assistance or a listening ear, she is there making a contribution. Such is her giving nature, that even strangers are automatically drawn to her, to whom they express their woes.

It is important to realise, when interacting with others in your daily existence, that every action or reaction that emanates from you impacts fundamentally on the life of another. We do not live in a vacuum. Sometimes when we act out or against something in our lives, it is difficult to foresee the ramifications of those actions. But try we must, because if we fail to, in the long run we could do more damage to ourselves and others than we could ever imagine. A child dies through the thoughtless action of a drunk driver, a mother's life stops in her despair; a child dies through the negligence of her carer, a father's life is dedicated to the advocacy of children's rights; a brilliant young woman is denied the right to study medicine, because of lack of access to sponsorship, a generation of people are denied access to a life saving new cancer drug which would have been developed by that brilliant young woman. Lives are destroyed or made by the actions or inaction of others.

I remember an experience that I had a few years ago, in which I was driving through the western coast of Namibia and picking up people along the way giving them a ride, as and when I could. I did this because I could, it certainly cost me nothing to do so. Therefore, I had no reason to resist even had I wanted to. I had a dear companion with me on my journey and on the way back home from our long trip, my friend asked me quite angrily, why had I picked up so many people, allowed so many into my vehicle for long journeys, without taking money from them? I stated that there was no reason for me to have taken money from what appeared to be poor people. The conversation became very heated and eventually I asked of my devout Christian friend, 'had not the Black Messiah (known as Jesus Christ in my friend's spiritual belief system) given unconditionally, asking for nothing in return for his teachings and miracles?' She became confused at this question, replying 'you are not Jesus. It is not the same thing.' Eventually she stumbled as we became more deeply involved in our conversation, and wanted to move away from the analogy with Jesus. I could not get her to accept that we are all children of God, who have the ability to act in the image of God, giving of ourselves, expecting nothing in return.

If you believe that Jesus lived, or that Muhammad lived, or that any person lived who sought to bring good to the world all the days of their life on earth, you must believe that you too have the capacity to live giving of the spirit. Your reward for this will be more than you ever imagined possible.

Spirit works for us in many ways, for when we are at our lowest ebb, we may want to just run and hide, and try our best to bury the problem that has led to our feelings of despondency and fear. But this is the worst thing that we could possibly do. We may feel like licking our wounds in solitude and forget the circumstances that led to those feelings, but what we really need to do is look at the issues which led to these feelings, in a spirit of openness and a willingness to effect change. When feeling down, the best thing to do is not run from our spiritual self, but rather run towards it. Use our spiritual self as a foundation to build a more secure life for ourselves.

Often times, people come to a fuller understanding of themselves when they are faced with issues concerning their faith. It is not necessary to be 'religious' to experience this. We all believe in something and our faith can be shaken by the circumstances of our lives. When this happens and we are plunged into the valley of seemingly never ending hurt and questions, we may not know what to do. At times like these, the best thing you can do is hold on to your faith in life and renew your spirit. Valley dwelling is not eternal, we all rise eventually. A valley can only exist if there are mountain tops to be navigated. It is only natural that when we cross from one peak in our lives to another that we will need to walk through the valley. No hue-man being has yet developed the capability to fly from one mountain top to the next. So valleys are not to be feared, but to be understood in their proper context and to be used as a low foundation from which to launch ourselves into the high altitudes, atop the mountain.

Recognise that
- The valley never appears so deep when you are in unison with the inner spirit, for your flexible and bottomless spirit will galvanise you out of the depths in which we all find ourselves at some point in time.
- The feeding of our spirits while we are in the valley will only serve to make change less painful.
- You were created from spirit and therefore you must live from your core, which is spirit, in order to get the best from life.
- In living from the spirit you do not become vulnerable, but rather you are strengthened.
- Spirit gives a sense of peace, sometimes difficult to find in the hustle and bustle of life.
- When you hit the valley, as we all do, give yourself an opportunity to rest, to re-charge your batteries and to evaluate your life.

Self-affirmation
- I live from my spirit.
- I feed my spirit through meditation, at which time I seek guidance on the things that concern me, the answers to which lie dormant inside of me.
- I greet each day with love in my heart for myself, and my sistahs and brothas.
- I give whenever I can, for it costs me nothing.
- I listen to my spirit at all times.

This Bridge Named My Back

I walk tall….most of the time
I look direct…
well every now and again at least.
I try hard, real hard….
that is until I get tired
which is often these days.

I have direction in all that I do
that is some of the time
at least until I get distracted,
disillusioned or hurt.
I do believe in myself…
that is I try to believe in myself,
my strength of character
and loving determination.
But sometimes……
often times I let distrust in
when she knocks, kicking at my door.
I let her in, because I have a kind heart.
I do not like to leave
my sistah outside in the cold.
I want to bring her in and comfort her.

I still have not learnt
how to hold her disbelief at bay,
calm her fears, awaken her desires,
give life to her dreams and aspirations.

I try hard, when I am alert,
which is 80 per cent of the time,
to keep the destroyers at bay.
Which is better than most.
I am not always successful,
but I try….damn hard.

I guess the next stage, is
learning how to love my wayward sistah
who lies dormant within me,

waiting to expose my weaknesses.
Yes, I must learn to love her better.
Perhaps then she will realise.
She is me
I am her
We are one.
Only then can we stop pulling against each other
for this one soul called Afrika.

Chapter 18

Epilogue: New Awakenings

In these times of the destruction of Afrikan civilisation and Afrikan peoples; in these times of the destruction of the earth's stratosphere; in these times of greater moves, by lesser people, to alter the minds of Afrikan people; in these times of the increased criminalisation of Afrikan youth, the best offensive position open to us is the furthering of our people through the furthering of our minds. Many constraints exist in the minds of Afrikan people. All over the world, some of us perceive of ourselves as a people in bondage, people who cannot make it, cannot get up and get out of the disheartening situations in which we find ourselves. Some of us have come to accept those constraints as bonds that cannot be broken. This is, of course untrue. There remain many instances in which we can make positive contributions to the communities in which we live, and to our own families.

Today, although we live in a world which has more resources and technology at its disposal than ever before, still we find hue-man beings living in poverty. At this point in time, it should seem strange to us that there is such a thing called poverty in the midst of so much wealth. Why is it easier to spend billions of dollars sending a few privileged people into space, yet seem inconceivable to better the lives of millions of people on this planet, living in abject poverty? Our minds have been so altered by the propaganda of those that control the world that we find it easier to conceive of visiting another planetary system than we do improving the one in which we live. I know I am not alone in thinking that there is something dreadfully wrong with this picture. But it is not enough to lament the world in which we find ourselves. We should be doing something towards making a positive contribution towards its renaissance, in line with what we as Afrikans see as a more positive world.

Generally, one of the biggest problems facing the Afrikan is the sometimes lack of creativity and initiative, which we are comfortable to display. Sometimes when we see that things are clearly wrong, we cannot comprehend how to change them for the better. We are so compartmentalised in our thinking of the things that affect us that when our communities stand as breeding grounds for disease and decay, we await some mysterious or otherwise external figure, like the State, to come and clean it up, rather than use our own *initiative* and effect the changes that we want in our environment for ourselves. The malaise of the western conceptualisation of the state has been so destructive that we now find it difficult to do even the smallest thing for ourselves. If the state has not cleaned the drains in two decades, they are unlikely to start doing so tomorrow, so what are you going to do about it. In so many towns throughout Afrika, one finds still stagnant waters festering in our communities, due to blocked drains filled with rubbish. These act as breeding grounds for mosquitoes and other disease infected insects to plague and kill our children. In the inner cities of Black designated areas in Europe and the Americas, we find rubbish tips and drug dens forming next door, acting as adventure playgrounds for our unsuspecting children. Instead of forming collective community task forces of the concerned and unemployed, to clean up the mess that affects all of us, we allow it to remain, in the hope that somehow, somewhere, somebody else will take on board the task. But recent history shows us that it is not going to happen. *We are the greatest catalyst for change.* If we can get up and do for self, we will be a long way on the road to re-establishing a great Afrikan civilisation, in the tradition of our Ancestors. The Afrikan women as the backbone of the family and as the most intuitive intelligent force must take a prominent role in bringing about change for the betterment of all Afrikans.

As Sistahs, we must all challenge ourselves and each other to reach the mountaintop. Know yourself, and encourage yourself to reach for excellence. Know that you have an infinite capacity for greatness. Know that nothing is beyond your reach. The only way for us is up. All other roads lead only to mediocrity. Act as the perfect role model for yourself and others, especially for the children in your life. In so doing, you will give yourself and the children that you can influence the right start in life.

Remember, strong Afrikan woman, that you are a blessing, never a curse. You are the greatest life force there is on the face of this earth. Through your womb all that can be good flows forth. So keep challenging yourself to reach those heights, so that you might pass your knowledge and wisdom on to those worthy of following in your exalted footsteps.

These words I share with you in a spirit of peace and love.

Notes

Notes

Notes

Notes